Balancing Act

The Young Person's Guide to a Career in Chemical Engineering

Dr. Bradley James Ridder

"The only easy day was yesterday."

-U.S. Navy SEALS motto

1.1.2 Table of Contents

1 Introduction and Biography

1.1 Introduction

"But I don't want to go among mad people," Alice remarked.
"Oh, you can't help that," said the Cat: "we're all mad here. I'm mad. You're mad."
"How do you know I'm mad?" said Alice.
"You must be," said the Cat, "or you wouldn't have come here."

-Lewis Carroll, *Alice in Wonderland*

The end of high school and the years beyond it are a special time in a young person's existence, where there appear to be infinite possibilities of what life may hold in store. There is also the burdensome task of choosing a career for oneself. Some choose the military. Some waste their twenties on menial jobs, chasing love interests, or playing video games. Some choose college, but party and drink their way through it. A small, intelligent, doughty lot go into engineering and the hard sciences. This last path is what concerns us in this book, specifically related to chemical engineering.

When faced with such an enormous number of possible paths, it helps to have a mentor to give advice. I did not have such a person to help me, and had to roll with the punches. No one in my immediate family has a degree in the hard sciences or engineering, much less a PhD. It was truly uncharted territory for me, and often times, I did not know what to expect or what the future portended. *Balancing Act* is the distillation – no pun intended – of my eleven years of schooling in the subject of chemical engineering obtained at the University of South Florida and Purdue University in West Lafayette, Indiana. I wrote this book to serve as a guide to all aspects of chemical engineering school, and not just the academics. Some of the advice comes from tactics that paid off. Other advice comes from a hard knock on the head. I hope it serves you well.

1.2 Why Write *Balancing Act?*

"Engineers like to solve problems. If there are no problems handily available, they will create their own problems."

-Scott Adams

I wrote *Balancing Act* because I felt that many of the problems I encountered during my studies could have been avoided with some simple advice. However, a search on Amazon revealed a paucity of books dealing with the subject. The reader might wonder, "Why not write a 'general' book on engineering school? Wouldn't that be more useful, and make your book more applicable to the general audience?" My opinion is of course, "No!" There are three reasons for this.

For one, chemical engineering is my true field of expertise. I only have second-hand knowledge about what most other engineering specialties do, other than very obvious things (e.g. civil engineers build bridges and roads, and that mechanical engineers like to design shafts). With this route, I would have ended up with a pile of superficial knowledge about other engineering disciplines, with the only real knowledge contributions coming from my personal experiences. Giving this book more mass appeal would have led to a watered-down text that no one would want to read, rather than a smaller number of people wanting to read.

Secondly, a general text would likely be so large that no one would read it, since engineering in its totality is such an enormous subject. The audience is not "chemical engineers," the audience is "people interested in learning more about chemical engineering." Anyone interested in engineering to begin with is probably looking for guidance as to which engineering specialty they should pursue, with hopefully more information backing their choice than starting salary figures. This book's purpose is to provide that information specifically with regards to chemical engineering.

Thirdly, I am personally of the opinion that chemical engineering is special among the other engineering disciplines, requiring a greater deal of finesse, care, and attention when discussing the subject to a lay person. It is fairly obvious what civil engineers do. They build bridges, buildings, dams, and other such infrastructure. Likewise, electrical engineers design circuits and electrical power systems. And so on for aerospace engineers, mechanical engineers, and even petroleum engineers. This diffusion of understanding into the consciousness of the general public does not exist for the chemical engineering profession. I cannot tell you how many times I have told someone I was a chemical engineering student, only to have them look at me with a blank stare and ask something to the effect of "So what do you guys actually do anyways? Play with chemicals?" Most people do not have the foggiest idea as to what chemical engineers do in practice, which might explain why so few decide upon it as a career choice.

There are several reasons for this widespread public ignorance. Chemical engineering knowledge is often mathematically dense, making it difficult for laypersons to grasp the important challenges in the field. Other engineering professions do not require an immense breadth of understanding of mathematics to grasp the basic idea, and produce goods and services with concrete applications, such as bridges, automobiles, or airplanes. There are obvious challenges and improvements that could be made with regards to those technologies, such as cars polluting less, planes moving faster, and bridges being built stronger. These technologies and their applications are encountered more on a daily basis in public life than for technologies germane to chemical engineering. How many members of the general public have the vaguest conception as to how petroleum is refined into gasoline or petrochemicals? Or how a biotechnology plant operates? How frequently do members of the general public interact with such entities? Hardly ever.

This lack of understanding is compounded by the immense breadth of the profession. Chemical engineers are involved in fields ranging from petroleum refining and chemicals manufacture, to designing new pharmaceutical drugs, math-based decision making, investment portfolio optimization, the extraction of natural gas and petroleum, the design of electrical power plants, and the design of new plastics, biomaterials, and advanced composites for all sorts of purposes. Many of the challenging problems in the field require significant breadth and depth of knowledge to understand, and can seem abstract and "far out there." One of the goals of *Balancing Act* is to communicate what chemical engineers actually do in a way understandable to a bright young person, without watering down the material so much that no actual learning takes place.

1.3 Brief Autobiography

"A journey of a thousand miles begins with a single step."

-Lao Tze, The Tao Te Ching

I grew up in Spring Hill, Florida, a small town in Hernando Coun-
ty not worth expending much energy talking about. The town was economically depressed, and there were virtually no opportunities for a
young person there. The people who amounted to something in school
either joined the military or went to college. Those who stayed behind
usually got involved with crystal meth or oxycodone, and pretty much
ruined their lives.

As a boy, I often found it very difficult to "click" with other people, and didn't have many friends growing up. I hated Boy Scouts, and
never really got involved in after school activities. Church was OK, but
not all of it was my cup of tea. I was never much of a troublemaker as a
kid. I've never been arrested, and only once got sent to the principal's
office in elementary school. I really enjoyed video games and art, and at
one point wanted to be a concept artist for a video game studio. Before
the eleventh grade, I never really considered myself a "good" student. I
was the kind of guy who would slack off until the last minute, read the
course material the day before the exam, and be happy with getting a
"B." I even got a "C" in Algebra 1.

I grew up in a high-conflict household. My mother and father
would fight frequently – usually over money. I hated it. In hindsight,
my father was probably mentally ill. He would be happy and content
one moment, and then would fly into an abusive, uncontrollable rage in
an instant. Several times the police had to be called to our house to get
his violent temper under control. There was no telling what misstep
would set him off. He was bitterly resentful about being drafted during
Vietnam War, and took out much of his frustrations with the federal
government on his own family.

My dad had little formal education, and could never hold down a
job. The only qualification he had going for him was his training in
communications from when he got drafted into the Army. As a boy I
saw my father nearly always unemployed, and would fruitlessly pray
that he would finally one day get a steady job. At times he would come
up with ridiculous ideas on how to make a fast buck, or get something

for nothing. He bought a computer for himself when I was in elementary school, with the intent of becoming a software developer. That stupid computer was the source of endless fights, since my dad spent what little money he had left from his last good job on buying it. Of course, he did not have the education or know-how to do that kind of work, and quickly gave up on it. Then he tried to apply for disability with the federal government, and of course, being perfectly able-bodied, was rejected. He would routinely call his brothers on the phone to beg for money, and would become enraged when they would refuse. I don't blame them; I wouldn't have given him my hard-earned money either.

My father's unemployment affected me deeply. I developed a fatalistic attitude about how my life was going to turn out. I was afraid that no matter what I did, I was going to wind up penniless, angry, and bitter just like Dad. It all sounds so silly in retrospect, but as a kid, I didn't know any better. I wondered if maybe it wasn't really Dad's fault, and that maybe it was just incredibly difficult to get a job. As time went on though, it became apparent that he was just a lazy bum who didn't want to work for a living. Plenty of my friends' dads all had jobs, but mine didn't.

Matters reached a nadir when I was a teenager. I started telling myself "I have to get out of this place." When I was grown up and had my own wife and children, I never wanted those awful arguments to take place in my house. I felt that if I made enough money, and there was plenty to go around, there would never be any need to fight over it. With enough money, everyone would be able to have their basic needs and reasonable wants fulfilled. I knew I needed to find a career field where unemployment wasn't a problem, and wages were high. Anything to fix the problem.

I signed up for Advanced Placement Chemistry with Mrs. Vonada going into my junior year of high school. I was shocked at how unprepared I was for the course. This was essentially a real college-level class, but available in high school. It was an extremely difficult, uphill battle. I never had to study so much before for any class. I still remember having to get up at 5:00 AM to get to school and work on labs for the course. Long story short, I passed the AP Chemistry exam with a 4. I had proven to myself that I could handle a real college-level science course.

My experiences in AP Chemistry disabused me at how far behind I was academically compared to many of my classmates. Other students in the program had 4.0 or above-4.0 grade point averages going into their junior and senior years. I had a measly 3.5. Some had read at significant breadth and depth beyond their regular class work. I was utterly disillusioned with my prior academic performance when a good friend of mine in the AP program won a summer research internship at the Massachusetts Institute of Technology writing computer codes to process data from radio telescopes. I was blown away that such an opportunity even existed, let alone that I was in no position to obtain it. My performance in freshman and sophomore years was too weak, and I had no significant extra-curricular involvement, nor any accomplishments of note outside of school. I began viewing most my life before the age of sixteen as purely a waste of time. I knew I had to do better.

But I learned from my mistakes. Getting involved with the AP program set me on a very positive track in life. Instead of hanging out with deadheads in easier classes, I was in the same classes with kids who were certainly going places. I learned the importance of working hard and studying seriously. I also learned the value of going beyond the coursework, being a self-motivated learner, and independently studying related material on my own. My self-esteem greatly improved, as I was doing well on the tests. The harder and longer I studied, the easier things became. My classmates started coming to me for help. I felt good about myself in a way I had never really thought possible.

I began realizing I was much more capable than I'd originally thought, so going into my senior year of high school I signed up for five AP courses. Senior year was tough, but I look back fondly on those times. I made many good friends, and we had a lot of fun that year hanging out. I remember studying for Mr. Davenport's physics class so much, I thought my head would explode. I ended up passing all five of those exams, and my self-confidence soared. I felt like I had unlimited potential, and could accomplish anything I set my mind to.

I took the SAT twice during my senior year of high school. The first time I got a 1240 on it. It was a respectable score, but not what I wanted. As penance, I studied vocabulary with great diligence, got some prep books, and worked math problems. I also forgot to bring my glasses the first time I took the test, and couldn't see the clock to keep up with how much time I had left. I had to assume the worst, and plowed through the exam without marshaling my available time effectively. The extra studying – and bringing my glasses – paid off handsomely the second go-around. The second time I took the SAT, I got a 1470: a 700 on the math, and a 770 on the verbal.

BALANCING ACT

During my senior year of high school (fall 2003 to spring 2004), I thought long and hard about what I wanted to do in life. I researched all sorts of different college majors. Considering the war in Iraq had only started a few months[1] prior, and being sent to the front-line was practically guaranteed, I crossed the military off my list of potential careers. I had a scholarship to go to college, so why risk getting blown up? I knew medical doctors made lots of money, but medicine had never interested me. Several of my friends in high school were already dead-set on going to college and majoring in the sciences or engineering, so there was always much talk about the subject. I felt that engineering school was what I wanted to do in college, but which kind of engineering I wasn't immediately sure about.

I really enjoyed AP Chemistry in my junior year, and was enjoying AP Physics and AP Calculus in my senior year. In light of those observations, I decided to investigate chemical engineering. I began searching on Monster.com for what jobs were available to people with chemical engineering degrees. It was a pretty straightforward decision after that. Salaries were being posted for $80,000, $90,000, and even over $100,000 a year for chemical engineers with the sufficient experience level and specialized background. The jobs sounded exciting and technically challenging. It sounded like a win-win.

I began attending the University of South Florida in Tampa in the fall of 2004. Despite the school not being highly ranked, I found the education extremely challenging. I spent countless hours during those years at the library or the engineering study center reading, doing homework, and going over previous coursework. I made it a goal of mine to get A's in every class. I failed at that quest, but I came close. I felt I had truly hit my stride in college. I finished my undergraduate studies *summa cum laude*.

I became interested in research during my time in the program, and considered going on to graduate school. After my senior year, I decided to get a master's degree at USF, to "test the waters" in case I wanted to get a PhD. I worked in the (now defunct) Applied Surface Science and Kinetics Laboratory working on catalysts for treating polluted wastewater. During that time, I familiarized myself with the subfield of process systems engineering, which influenced the direction I would take for my PhD. My professors strongly encouraged me to go

---

[1] March 20, 2003 was the commencement of hostilities according to Wikipedia.

on and get a PhD. I applied to multiple programs across the country. Eventually, I settled on doing a PhD at Purdue University in West Lafayette, Indiana. It was a heck of a ride. My PhD project was on the application of mathematical optimization methods to improving the production of pharmaceutical drug crystals. After five years of hard work, I finished my PhD in the Spring of 2015. Now I live and work in Milwaukee, Wisconsin applying those same mathematical optimization methods to improving large air conditioning processes.

1.4 Benediction

"Only a fool learns from his own mistakes. The wise man learns from the mistakes of others."

-Otto von Bismarck

The goal of this book is not to "sell" chemical engineering, as if I were a used car salesman hawking lemons to suckers. The purpose is to give you all the facts – and fact-supported opinions – necessary to draw your own conclusions. If you decide chemical engineering is a good fit for you, then welcome to the club. If, after reading this book, you decide it isn't, then the book has still succeeded. Many students are, at least initially, attracted to chemical engineering simply due to the high starting pay. This is being penny wise, but pound foolish. It is not worth it to major in a subject you end up despising simply for a perhaps 10% increase in starting pay. There is no shortage of choices in other engineering fields, such as civil, electrical, mechanical, aerospace, biological, biomedical, industrial, petroleum, and computer engineering, as well as computer science. While not specifically listed as "engineering" majors, actuarial science and operations research are also very math-intensive. Even if chemical engineering is unsatisfactory for you, there is certainly another STEM[2] sub-field that may be a good fit.

My hope is that this book will not only steer bright young minds towards chemical engineering as a career, but also help to them avoid many of the potholes and pitfalls I encountered – or successfully avoided – that can stymie their advancement. Much of the discussion in this book also applies to biomedical engineers and biological engi-

---

[2] Science, Technology, Engineering, and Mathematics

neers, as the educations are similar. Ultimately though, no book can completely prepare someone for engineering school. Your school will be different from mine. Your motivations will be different from mine. Your professors will be different. Your fellow students will be different. Your personal dreams and ambitions will be different, and all of these factors will influence your correct course of action. All I can do is offer as much friendly advice from my own experiences as I can. The rest will be up to you.

I think this where I am supposed to wish my reader "good luck." Luck, however, is a minuscule part of the equation. Despite the platitudes and clichés echoed in the popular press, no one in the history of mankind has ever been given an education. If you want an education, get off your rear end and take it. We live in the Internet Age, where Wikipedia, Google, and Amazon can supply most practical information needs. Your college will have a well-stocked library, with plenty of chairs and seats for you to plop into and study. It's all up to you, and no one else. You have the power in your hands and the brains in your head to change the path of your life to a productive, rewarding one. Your choices, and the consequences following from them, good or bad, are completely in your control. Luck has nothing to do with that.

-Dr. Bradley James Ridder

Milwaukee, Wisconsin

January 16, 2016

2 What is Chemical Engineering?

2.1 Hard Questions

"Judge a man by his questions rather than his answers."

-Voltaire

Imagine you walk into the office at your job, and you get an email phrased like one of the following:

- "Hi Joe. The Automotive Fuels Division wants us to investigate a new catalyst computationally before they bother synthesizing it. Have a plan for how you'll write up the computer program for doing this by the end of the week. Give us some numbers and uncertainties on expected turnover frequencies for them. Also provide an estimate on the amount of computer time you'll need on the cluster. "

- "We need to design a process that can produce spherical polymer particles of uniform size and shape. The client tells us the smaller the particles are, the more profitable they are to sell. The pilot-plant data for producing fifty kilograms an hour is attached in the email. We need to scale-up to five tons an hour."

- "Our market research survey indicates that consumers would be particularly interested in buying bandages that automatically become warm and then cold after being applied to a wound. Write a plan of attack on the design of this product by the end of the week. We'll need a full write-up on product requirements, safety issues, costs, and production volume. Of course, we can't use any toxic substances in this product. Furthermore, the market research says most people won't pay more than $10 for fifty such bandages."

- "A group of venture capitalists has contacted us. They are pondering investing another round of funding into an entrepreneur's new technology for producing automotive-grade diesel from sugarcane biomass. The inventor claims that he is ready to take the technology to the pilot-scale, but will need $2 million of investment capital to make it happen. We're putting you on a flight to meet with this fellow and view the bench-scale setup. We want you to prepare a report for the investors on the likely performance of his new technology at both the pilot and mass-production scales. None of these investors are technical people, but they want to know if this technology is sound. Don't forget about those new EPA regulations that went into effect last year – if his process pollutes too much, they'll just shut it down."

- "A major university is spending a fortune each year on electricity costs. They've built a new cogeneration plant for converting natural gas into electricity and useful heat. They're interested in upgrading their control systems in the plant to get more efficiency. You have background in thermodynamics and controls, so we're handing this one to you. I want to be able to tell them we can save them $1 million a year – but of course, be honest in your analysis. Let us know what data you need and what experiments the plant personnel will need to run for you, and we'll see if we can work something out."

- "We just got more details on that new government contract. The military is putting out a request for bids for a company to destroy 5,000 tons of chemical weapons within four years. The process cannot produce worse pollutants than the weapons are, and leakage of the weapons is obviously unacceptable. Declassified technical details of the weapons are attached in the email. We need to come up with a process for destroying these weapons that satisfies the environmental requirements and gives us at least 20% profit. We need as low a bid as possible to have a chance at winning the contract."

2.2   A Working Definition of Chemical Engineering

"One man's 'magic' is another man's engineering. 'Supernatural' is a null word."

-Robert A. Heinlein

As can be seen by these examples, chemical engineers solve all sorts of interesting and diverse problems, under a variety of time frames, size scales, and economic and technical constraints. Often, they don't have or know ahead of time all the data they will need to execute a project, or how much effort it will require to completely define and solve the problem. They are also held to high levels of ethical responsibility, as people ignorant of the subject will often be guided by the engineer's opinions. Such is the life of the humble chemical engineer, by whose intellect civilization endures. Were it not for the Haber[3] process[4] for the production of ammonia, billions would starve [2]. Were it not for advanced materials, your computer hard drive would be a paperweight. Were it not for the refining of petroleum, your gas tank would be empty, and you'd be hoofing it everywhere. And so on for countless other technological wonders we take for granted in our modern society.

Back to the question asked in the chapter title: what is chemical engineering? A broad definition is:

Chemical engineering is the application of mathematics, physics, and chemistry to the transformation of matter and energy for useful human purposes in the safest and most efficient manner possible.

This is accomplished by designing large chemical processing plants, improving existing processes, and developing new chemical products. All sorts of industrial reactions are necessary for the modern products we use everyday, such as alkylations for the production of

---

[3] Fritz Haber was a German chemist. During the First World War, he was highly nationalistic and worked ardently on chemical weapons for the German government. In one of history's cruel ironies, Haber invented a deadly gas called Zyklon B, which was used in the death camps during the Holocaust. Haber himself was of Jewish ethnicity. He died in exile in Switzerland in 1934, hated by his country.

[4] The Haber process is the production of ammonia from nitrogen and hydrogen. Mass production began in the 1920's [1]. Ammonia is a key feedstock in fertilizer production.

fuels, to sulfonations, fluorinations, chlorinations, hydrogenations, the steam reforming of methane, and the water-gas shift reaction [3]. Chemical reactions are used to manufacture most of the important substances we take for granted in everyday life, such as fuels, construction materials, textiles, plastics and polymers, and metals. Odds are, if you can name a technology, its chemical processing had a direct impact on its performance [4].

Chemical engineers employ a diverse arsenal of scientific and mathematical tools for solving problems in this domain. The building blocks of understanding are algebra, calculus, and differential equations. Many phenomena in chemical engineering are random processes and require the use of probability and statistics to model. Sensitive instrumentation is used to investigate chemical systems, such as atomic force microscopy, scanning-electron microscopy, confocal microscopy, ellipsometry, x-ray diffraction, x-ray photo-electron spectroscopy, neutron scattering, infrared spectroscopy, electron dispersion spectroscopy, and nuclear magnetic resonance. High-performance computers are used for solving large systems of equations that would be intractable for a human to solve, and also for visualization of the phenomena being studied. Computers are helpful at modeling and investigating the interplay between chemical reactions and the transport equations of mass, momentum, and energy. These are the basic tools of problem solving the world of chemical engineering.

2.3 A Brief History of Chemical Engineering

"The engineer has been, and is, a maker of history."

-James Kip Finch

Chemical engineering as a discipline is new compared to other engineering fields [5]. Mechanical and civil engineering have their origins with the pharaohs of ancient Egypt, while chemical engineering appeared only after the birth of the chemicals industry in the late nineteenth century [2], [5]. The earliest practical applications of chemistry are the fermentation of alcoholic beverages and the distillation of alcohol [5]. High demand for the chemical engineering profession came from the mining, agricultural, and textile industries [6]. By 1880, the mass production of chemicals was in full swing across the developed world. The development of the petroleum and agrochemical industries provided great impetus to the establishment of chemical engineering as a specialty. In particular, the petrochemical, polymer, semiconductor, and biotechnology industries experienced large growth after the Second World War [3]. The development of high-performance computing technologies has revolutionized all fields of engineering, especially chemical engineering. Today, computers can be used to design chemical processing equipment, for process scale-up, and for solving difficult mathematical problems in the field.

2.4   Industries and Companies That Employ Chemical Engineers

"A human being should be able to change a diaper, plan an invasion, butcher a hog, conn a ship, design a building, write a sonnet, balance accounts, build a wall, set a bone, comfort the dying, take orders, give orders, cooperate, act alone, solve equations, analyze a new problem, pitch manure, program a computer, cook a tasty meal, fight efficiently, die gallantly. Specialization is for insects."

-Robert A. Heinlein

It is impossible to exhaustively list all of the industries that employ chemical engineers, since the versatility of the education makes a chemical engineer fit for almost any technically demanding occupation. Some go on to become movie directors, patent attorneys, Wall Street quants[5] , the chairmen of major corporations[6] , entrepreneurs, and even astronauts[7] . More commonly, chemical engineers are employed in the chemicals industry and the energy sector. Many prestigious Fortune 500 companies employ chemical engineers [8]. Table 1 below summarizes representative industries and companies that employ chemical en-

---

[5] "Quant" is short for "quantitative analyst." Quants use sophisticated mathematics to make strategic bets on the price movements of financial instruments.

[6] Andrew Grove was the founder of Intel, and Jack Welch ran General Electric from 1981 to 2001.

[7] Mae Jemison was the first black female astronaut. She has a Bachelor's in Chemical Engineering from Stanford University, and a doctorate of medicine from Cornell University [7].

gineers, ranked by worldwide revenue. Clearly, the petroleum and pharmaceutical industries are extraordinarily well off, though all of these industries are enormous.

Table 1: Industries and companies that employ chemical engineers.

Industry	Representative Companies	Worldwide Industry Annual Revenues (billions of dollars)	References
Petroleum and natural gas	Chevron, Exxon Mobil, Sinopec, British Petroleum, Saudi Aramco	4000-5750	[9], [10]
Pharmaceuticals	Roche, Novartis, Merck, Bayer, AbbVie, Ranbaxy	1000-1300	[11], [12]
Processed food	Archer-Daniels-Midland, ConAgra Foods	575	[13]
Pulp and paper	International Paper Company, Kimberly-Clark	567	[14]
Metallurgy, mining, and metal extraction	BHP Billiton, Rio Tinto, Glencore, Mosaic, Barrick Gold	453	[15], [16]
Electric power (natural gas, coal, nuclear, etc.)	Duke Energy, Pacific Gas and Electric, Consolidated Edison	375	[17], [18]
Medical devices	Johnson and Johnson, Medtronic, General Electric, Siemens, Stryker	350	[19], [20]
Household products	Unilever, Procter and Gamble, Kimberly-Clark	120	[21]
Plastics and polymers	Dow Chemical, Celanese Chemicals	108	[22], [23]

2.5 Chemistry vs. Chemical Engineering

"Engineers use knowledge primarily to design, produce, and operate artifacts. Scientists, by contrast, use knowledge primarily to generate more knowledge."

-Walter Vincenti

Many people wonder what the difference is between "chemists" and "chemical engineers." There is an important distinction between them. Chemists typically work at the lab-scale or bench-scale, while chemical engineers work with chemical processes at the production scale. Producing a few milligrams of a substance in three hours is very different from producing tons of it per day. This regime shift greatly changes the types of processes required for profitable manufacturing. Chemists are also far more science and research-focused. Chemists, and scientists in general, add to the knowledge pool, while engineers draw from it [6].

Education-wise, there are significant differences between the chemistry and chemical engineering curricula. Chemists study and memorize large libraries of chemical reactions, and also study some of the fundamental theories behind the existence of chemical reactions (e.g. statistical and quantum mechanics). Chemical engineers however, study the practical implementation of various reaction schemes, and how the various transport phenomena (e.g. fluid flow, chemical diffusion, and heat transfer) affect the outcome of a reaction. There is significantly more mathematics in a chemical engineering undergraduate degree than in a chemistry one. Chemists also study in greater detail the workings and theory behind the various tools they use for chemical analysis, especially the various spectroscopy instruments.

A comparison of representative chemistry and chemical engineering course plans is instructive [24], [25]. Mathematics for a chemistry major generally stops at calculus II, which is probably all that is needed to understand the higher-level theoretical chemistry courses. A chemical engineer however, will take many more mathematically-intensive courses after that (e.g. calculus III, differential equations, statistics, transport phenomena, chemical thermodynamics, reaction engineering, and mass transfer). There would be virtually no study of chemical process control in a chemistry course, while it is an important consideration in the design of real chemical processes.

3 The Worth of a Chemical Engineering Degree

3.1 Your Best Bet

"An investment in knowledge pays the best interest."

- Benjamin Franklin

I'm going to get on my soapbox briefly, and explain to the reader how the world works from a high-level perspective. You see, friend, the fuel in the engine of our civilization is money. Some people have more of it than others. In fact, some people – usually gray, old members of the rentier class – have tons of it. People with lots of money are usually preoccupied with investing it, so as to grow their fortunes. These gray old men divert their fortunes into diversified investment funds, managed by investment professionals. These people in turn, invest that money into sectors of the economy they think are going to see growth. In this way, capital works its way throughout the economy. But where are those fund managers going to place their bets? Who are they going to trust with that money? Will it be in the industry in which you work, or somewhere else?

You have no control over where those gray old men bet their money, but your choice of college major is actually your own "bet." When you pick a college major, you're betting that your choice of degree is going to cause capital to flow towards you, and put money into your pocket. Chemical engineers are people to whom significant public and private capital will be directed to in the twenty-first century. I've met many people who have made a fortune for themselves doing chemical engineering. A few owned their own consulting companies. Some have gone on to become patent attorneys, and make over $300,000 a year. Some charge enormous hourly fees to act as expert witnesses during court proceedings. One fellow even had his own charitable foundation, with its endowment funded off the royalties from one of his patents. Another guy started his own chemical company in graduate school, flipped it, and retired at a young age. One wealthy professor I met in Scotland told me that he and his wife went skiing regularly in the Swiss Alps.

The easiest way to become wealthy is to live frugally, invest heavily, minimize tax payments using legal methods, and provide a useful good or service to entities who are already wealthy [26]–[28]. One straightforward way to do that in the twenty-first century is to learn a STEM trade and provide your skills to the technological economy. Chemical engineering is one of the most solid bets on STEM you can make. Money is needed to drive research and development, and there is great demand for new processes, materials, and products that require a chemical engineer's know-how to make. It will take chemical engineers to design and manage the plants that create those products. The U.S. fine chemicals industry alone is a $700 billion industry [29]. By going into chemical engineering, you can get yourself a small slice of a big pie.

3.2   The Stumbling Block of Worthless Degrees

"Why should fools have money in hand to buy wisdom, when they are not able to understand it?"

-The Old Testament, Proverbs 17:16

Your choice of college major is one of the most important decisions of your life, on par with your choice of spouse, choosing to have children, or getting a mortgage. Choose poorly, and you'll be relegated to a life of low-pay wage slavery. Choose wisely, and you'll live a life of relative comfort. The best bet you can make in college is a STEM major, which is more or less the last place you can go to get a rigorous education in the higher education system. An added bonus for pursuing a STEM degree is that STEM majors are generally free from the intense political indoctrination commonly encountered in the liberal arts.

Choosing a college major used to be a pretty straightforward affair back in the day – you simply majored in a subject that interested you and employment was more or less as assured. It does not work that way these days due to the proliferation of worthless degrees [30]. To be perfectly blunt, degrees in the liberal arts and humanities are financially poor decisions when viewed as financial investments, and are unlikely to produce returns that offset high student loan debt. Such degrees are of little help in securing a job, and do not offer any discernible benefits for entrepreneurial pursuits. They are quite literally worthless.

A strong indicator that a degree is worthless is that the degree-holders are not involved in the production of goods and services that people want to buy. Electrical and computer engineers design and build electronic components for computers. Chemical engineers are involved in the refining of petroleum. Mechanical engineers design and build automobiles, and the robots that make them. These are all products that people want to spend money on. What value is added to the economy by someone with a women's studies[8] or sociology degree? What goods or services do they produce? None! These kinds of degrees should be struck from your consideration immediately.

Chemistry degrees deserve a special mention. Several of my colleagues from undergraduate years were former chemistry majors or had a degree in chemistry, but were returning to school for chemical engineering because the pay was so much greater. Much of the analytical work in chemistry is automated now, greatly reducing the demand for chemists with only undergraduate qualifications. This is the main problem with the chemistry profession. Despite the great difficulty of the degree, chemists with only four-year qualifications are often stuck teaching high school. To really make it pay off, you have to get a PhD in chemistry and do chemical research for a living [31]. This problem extends to biology degrees as well.

3.3 Salaries and Benefits Enjoyed by Chemical Engineers

"Lazy hands make for poverty, but diligent hands bring wealth."

-The Old Testament, Proverbs 10:4

Chemical engineering serves as an archetype for degrees that are not worthless, especially when viewed from the angle of supply and demand. Chemical engineers are directly involved in the design and production of products that many people want to buy. Demand for

---

[8] A thought experiment: Who is involved in the design and mass production of better tampons, cosmetics, perfumes, birth-control pills, baby products, and sexual lubricants – the women's studies major, or the chemical engineer?

their skills is therefore high. Furthermore, comparatively few people have the intelligence, energy, and determination necessary to become a chemical engineer. Supply is therefore low. This is the law of supply and demand in action: supply is low and demand is high, so salaries are generally high.

The Bureau of Labor Statistics website is replete with data on chemical engineering salaries [32]. The median annual wage is about $96,000, and the mean starting salary (as of 2013) is $67,600 [33]. There is wide variance in these figures though. A friend of mine started off in the consumer products sector at $80,000. Another girl started off in the phosphate industry at $75,000. Petroleum engineers can make even more, starting off at approximately $93,000. One fellow I knew from Purdue graduated with his PhD from Purdue starting off at $110,000. Starting salaries vary significantly with the industry. Referring back to Table 1 oil and pharmaceutical companies generally offer top pay. Pay generally scales with your GPA, and many companies (e.g. Intel) have minimum cutoffs for GPA on their new hires.

Starting pay isn't everything though. Chemical engineering jobs can be quite cushy, with generous provisions for vacation days, paid time off, elective holidays, flexible work hours, and a relaxed work environment. Full medical benefits are practically standard. Retirement accounts (401k) generally have provisions for a company match, which is basically free money. Companies will bend over backwards to bring you on board if you have skills they desire, including paying for your move, helping you find a house, and paying the hotel bill for temporary lodging. One fellow I know who went into the oil industry lived in a nice hotel for a month with his wife and kids until they found permanent lodging. The oil company paid for it all. I was told by one girl who interviewed with an oil company that a pension was included in the benefits package, a benefit which in most other private industries has gone the way of the dinosaur[9].

In addition to their starting pay, chemical engineers can receive signing bonuses in the tens of thousand of dollars. As graduate students at Purdue, our annual stipends were approximately $26,000. A member of one of the catalysis research groups finished his PhD, and

---

[9] The only person I know of in the private sector who collected a pension was my grandfather, who was retired from Bethlehem Steel before he passed away in 1996. Bethlehem Steel went bankrupt in 2003.

was hired onto a position with an oil company. His signing bonus was greater than the annual stipend as a graduate student. Undergraduates at Purdue nearing graduation frequently had jobs waiting for them after graduation, and they too would get large signing bonuses.

Other benefits and perks depend on the occupation. If you go the research route and become a university professor, you can make about $125,000 per year. Top schools often pay much more. Additionally, if you are granted tenure, you cannot be fired unless you commit a felony, falsify research, the entire department gets shut down, or you have sex with one of your students. Research professors have almost complete freedom over what they study. One professor I spoke to during my PhD recruiting said outright, "The Howard Hughes Foundation said they don't really care what I do with the money." If you get a track record of winning research grants, universities will fight over you to join their faculty. There is risk going this route though. The granting of tenure is an "up or out" process. If you fail to make tenure within about five years, you will be fired.

3.4   Recruitment Methods by Private Industry

"I hire people brighter than me and then I get out of their way."

-Lee Iacocca

At USF and Purdue, tech companies aggressively recruited students from the engineering programs. Recruitment weeks were always a welcome treat at school, since it meant free food. Information sessions were almost always catered. Exponent, a top engineering consulting firm, bought full Jimmy John's meals for everyone. Intel bought enough Papa John's to feed a battalion while one of their top officers gave us a PowerPoint presentation on new positions being offered in the company. One company was giving out free boxes of a dozen doughnuts, just to listen to their recruiters at their booth. Not one doughnut – a whole box of them. They had a stockpile of doughnut boxes as tall as a man!

At Purdue, during company recruitment week, Mackey Basketball Arena was opened up to industry recruiters, and became packed with recruiting booths for Fortune 500 companies. The Stewart Center and Armstrong Hall hosted catered information sessions, where companies gave presentations on available jobs. There were always employers at Purdue looking to snap up top talent. If it weren't for the news media, you'd never have known there was a recession.

3.5 Recruitment Methods by Graduate Schools

"...to whom much is given, much will be required..."

-The New Testament, Luke 12:48

Top chemical engineering graduate schools are equally aggressive at recruiting the best students. I attended recruitment interviews at Northwestern University, Carnegie-Mellon University, Purdue University, and Notre-Dame University. The departments spared no expense.

During the recruitment session at Northwestern University in 2010, me and about twenty other prospective PhD students were treated like princes for a weekend. We were all flown out to Chicago, with transportation to the Orrington Hotel[10] , for free. We were treated to food at excellent restaurants, including a flat-top Mongolian grill and a Spanish tapas bar – the only rule was that they couldn't buy us alcohol with the department credit card. We were given one-on-one time with the graduate students, with no professors in sight, all so they could freely answer our questions without fear of reprisal. They were clear about which professors were jerks and to be avoided. One professor was unavailable to speak with us, since he was busy managing the affairs of his multi-million dollar technology start-up. On Saturday, we took the train out into Chicago from Evanston, walked the Magnificent Mile, saw the giant reflective bean, and had lunch on the top floor of the Hancock Building. I was personally told by a friend who was already in Northwestern's PhD program that the total bill for the recruitment weekend was over $35,000. The recruitment was especially aggressive at Northwestern, since the university's top brass were determined to make Northwestern an internationally renowned center for nanotechnology. And they looked to us to make it happen.

I had missed the main recruitment weekends at Carnegie-Mellon,

---

[10] Apparently, the Orrington Hotel has a long tradition with Northwestern University. I was asked by one of my professors at USF, who got his PhD thirty years ago at Northwestern, "Did they put you up in the Orrington Hotel too?"

but that didn't matter. They made a private recruitment weekend, just for me. They flew me out to Pittsburgh, had a private car drive me to and from the airport, and gave me one-on-one time with the professors I was interested in working with. All the professors were extraordinarily nice and polite, as were all the graduate students. I was shown the work areas, given one-on-one time with the graduate students, and was free to ask any questions I wanted. They were even nice enough to give me a Pittsburgh Steelers Terrible Towel for coming out and interviewing with them. I still have it.

Recruitment at Purdue was no joke either. Like the other universities, we were treated to all sorts of food, and put up in the Holiday Inn in West Lafayette. We were treated to nice restaurants, and the graduate students took us out to see the bar scene in West Lafayette. We also had a party at one of the graduate student's houses. As part of the research showcase, the graduate students from the department set up their research posters in the main atrium of the Forney Hall of Chemical Engineering. We were free to see all of the research being conducted at the school, and ask whatever questions we wanted.

My last stop during my recruitment odyssey was Notre-Dame in South Bend, Indiana. By this time, I was worn out from recruitment elsewhere. Not being Catholic, there was some culture shock. I saw a large shrine to the Virgin Mary outside, illuminated with an army of candles, girded with knee stools, with a flock of Catholic students genuflecting within the grotto. The recruitment weekend was generally more of the same. I got to meet the professors and graduate students, see the laboratories, and got treated to yummy food. During my last night in South Bend, I hung out with the graduate students, eating Papa Murphy's pizza and playing RISK in their apartment.

One of the best recruitment tools the top departments have is the pay. Being a graduate student in other disciplines is typically an awful ordeal. The pay is usually very low, making it a struggle to pay the bills and eat anything other than ramen. It wasn't that way at Purdue. Property is generally cheap in West Lafayette, and several graduate students at Purdue owned their own homes. One graduate student I knew at Purdue had his home built for him, after his wife had their two children. Several graduate students at Carnegie-Mellon also owned their own homes. I personally made significant progress in paying off my student loans. To reiterate, our annual stipend at Purdue was about $26,000, guaranteed for four years. I later learned we were the highest-paid graduate students at Purdue University. Not only did we get great pay, but also qualified for cheap graduate student health insurance with superb coverage. To quote one of my former colleagues: "I don't want for anything."

However, the competition for seats at these top programs is fierce. To give you an idea of what you're up against, I will reiterate my statistics. I had a 1490 GRE[11] score, and a 3.94 undergraduate GPA. I had won several awards during my time at USF. My team won the Best Process Design Award for our senior project, and I was voted Outstanding Senior for 2010 by the chemical engineering faculty. I had also distinguished myself in my classes, and my professors were forthcoming with recommendations to PhD programs. With these stats, I was rejected by MIT, CalTech, and Cornell University, and accepted to Northwestern, Carnegie-Mellon, Purdue, Notre-Dame, and Vanderbilt. My rejections from CalTech and Cornell were almost immediate, though MIT took a long time to reject me – presumably I was a "back up" in case someone they really wanted rejected their offer[12].

3.6   For Maximum Benefit, Graduate in Minimum Time

"At times it is folly to hasten; at other times, to delay. The wise do everything in its proper time."

-Ovid

The financial worth of any degree is greatly diminished the longer it takes you to get it. It took me four years to graduate with my bachelor's, and every semester was packed with difficult courses. I consider myself fortunate in this regard. Many of my undergraduate classmates took five or six years in college before they finally graduated with their bachelor's, either due to flunking classes or switching their major. Each additional year in college is a double loss: you aren't earning a salary,

---

[11]A high GRE score will not guarantee a seat. To quote one of my professors from USF: "A high score won't get you in, but a low score will keep you out." It's a filtering device.

[12] Yes, people actually do reject MIT for graduate school in chemical engineering. One professor I met during PhD recruitment had actually rejected MIT three times in his life: once for undergraduate, once for graduate school, and finally for a professorship.

and you have to take out more student loans. The worth of the degree is maximized only if you graduate in minimum time. Mathematically, any degree becomes worthless past a certain level of time and investment, even one as valuable as chemical engineering.

4 What Chemical Engineers Study in School

4.1 The Special Knowledge of Chemical Engineers

"An expert is one who knows more and more about less and less."

-Nicholas M. Butler

Chemical engineering rests upon an enormous body of knowledge necessary for the analysis and design of chemical processes. All engineers know a vast amount of mathematics, but the difference between the various engineering fields lies in what problems the math is applied to. In chemical engineering, the unique knowledge base by which chemical engineers solve problems includes [2], [5]:

- Material, energy, and momentum balances

- Chemical kinetics, catalysis, reactor design, and reaction engineering

- Biological systems

- Chemical thermodynamics

- Materials science

- Separation and purification technologies

- Process dynamics and control

- Process synthesis, product design, and optimization

- Economic analysis

4.2 The Material and Energy Balancing Act

"This is your last chance. After this, there is no turning back. You take the blue pill — the story ends, you wake up in your bed and believe whatever you want to believe. You take the red pill — you stay in Wonderland and I show you how deep the rabbit-hole goes."

-Laurence Fishburne, *The Matrix*

My undergraduate control systems professor, Dr. Joseph, once told us chemical engineers are "glorified plumbers." I actually would argue we are glorified accountants. Accountants all understand a single basic balance equation:

$$\frac{dP}{dt} = \dot{Y}_{in} - \dot{Y}_{out}$$

Where P is the profit, $\dot{Y}_{in}$ is the rate of money entering the business, $\dot{Y}_{out}$ is the rate money is leaving the business, and d/dt is a calculus term which means "the rate of change with respect to time." If the dP/dt term is negative, the business is losing money, and heads are sure to roll. Otherwise, the business is doing well, and can either reinvest the profits, increase its dividends to attract more investors, increase the pay of top corporate officers, or some combination thereof.

Virtually all of the chemical engineering body of knowledge rests upon accounting for where mass, energy, and momentum are going in a process [34], [35]. Instead of confining ourselves to a business, we chemical engineers regularly think of problems in terms of "control volumes." A control volume is a region of space demarcated by an invisible, incorporeal boundary. Within this boundary, we keep track of the amounts of mass, energy, and momentum entering and leaving the control volume. In the form of a differential equation, the general overall property balance is written as:

$$\frac{d\Phi}{dt} = \dot{\Phi}_{in} - \dot{\Phi}_{out} + \dot{\Phi}_{generated} - \dot{\Phi}_{consumed}$$

BALANCING ACT

The terms, in English, from left to right, starting across the equals sign, are described as:

1. The rate of a given property accumulated within the control volume.

2. The rate a given property enters the control volume.

3. The rate of the property leaving the control volume.

4. The rate of the property generated within the control volume.

5. The rate at which a property is consumed within the control volume.

This basic balance equation is the underpinning behind the analysis of all of the processes in the field of chemical engineering [5]. While the specific approach depends on the specific problem, the typical trajectory of problem-solving in chemical engineering goes something like this:

1. Write the material, energy, and momentum balance equations for the process.

2. State the assumptions needed to simplify the equations.

3. Solve the equations simultaneously.

Chemical engineers frequently encounter many different problems which utilize this basic trajectory, whether it is process control, product design, process optimization, economic feasibility studies, environmental impact studies, or researching new technologies. The same principles of property balances apply to the modeling of other complicated chemical processes. The methodology is independent of size scales, and the same physical principles that govern the behavior of a large chemical plant can be applied to the analysis of microscopic living cells, molecular motors, liquid droplets, and atmospheric dynamics [36], [37].

Material and energy balances are a big part of chemical engineering problem solving. They are used as the foundation for all further analysis and tasks in the field. If this sounds like an interesting concept to you, then chemical engineering might be a good fit. As a chemical engineer, you will be applying this strategy over and over again during your schooling and throughout the course of your career. If it sounds boring and uninteresting, then you might want to steer clear.

From a more general standpoint – applicable to pretty much every engineering discipline – most of engineering is solving equations such that $f(x) = 0$. This process is repeated over and over in engineering school, where large systems of equations are solved such that the right-hand side equals zero. If the entire idea of solving equations and doing math sounds unpalatable for you, run! Engineers love to solve equations and make the right-hand side zero!

4.3   The Core Sub-fields in Chemical Engineering

"The essence of the beautiful is unity in variety."

-Felix Mendelssohn

The core sub-fields in chemical engineering are all based upon material, energy, and momentum balances. We briefly discuss each sub-field here. In your education, you can expect to take at least one course in each of these subjects.

1. "Reaction engineering" concerns the design and analysis of chemical reactors, chemical catalysts, and the study of the kinetics of specific chemical reactions."Kinetics" refers to the rate at which reactants and products are consumed and formed. The study of reaction engineering is crucial, since a chemical reaction is not as simple as adding "A" and "B" together. The flow pattern of the two substances, mixing characteristics, and heat transfer rate strongly affect the reaction rate, selectivity, and yield of the desired products [3]. Catalysis is used in 95% of industrial chemical reactions, making this an important basic subject for any chemical engineer [38]. Biology is also utilized somewhat in reaction engineering, since some chemical products are manufactured using bioreactors and fermentation vats.

2. "Chemical thermodynamics" studies the equilibrium properties

of gases and liquids, especially mixtures of them. Also, thermo-dynamics can be used to investigate the scientific feasibility of chemical processes. Processes which produce or destroy energy are impossible, and processes that decrease the entropy of the universe are also impossible.

3. "Transport phenomena" is the study of the movement of mass, momentum, and energy through a medium due to a gradient in concentration, velocity, or temperature [34], [39]. It is common in manufacturing processes for fluid flow and heat transfer phenomena to impact the quality of the final product, hence the motivation for studying this subject. All three of these transport phenomena can occur at the same time, leading to exceedingly difficult mathematical modeling problems in chemical engineering.

4. "Separations design" involves, as its name implies, how to efficiently purify product streams. This is accomplished through a variety of equipment and processes, such as distillation columns, packed beds, solid leaching, hydrocyclones, gas stripping, liquid stripping, freeze-drying, and others.

5. "Process dynamics and control" studies how to automatically control chemical processes, subject to constraints on product quality and safety. Sophisticated computer models are often required for this purpose since chemical processes are often badly-behaved. It also studies the dynamic stability of control systems, which can be useful information for the design of a control system, and also impacts process safety.

6. "Process synthesis" is the study of how to design an entire chemical plant out of individual process units. Analysis of each individual unit operation is used to analyze the entire plant [5].

7. Finally, knowledge of "process economics and cost estimation" is required to calculate the bottom line. These calculations can become quite detailed, as chemical plants have long time horizons that can make profits susceptible to long-range uncertainty. Like my undergraduate plant design professor, Dr. Sunol,

31

said, "I don't care if you are solving partial differential equations – if you're changing expensive stuff into cheap stuff, you're going broke."

This knowledge base is not "compartmentalized" in practice. For example, separation of a petrochemical stream would require a holistic understanding of most of these bullet points. Knowledge of separation processes is needed to choose the correct technology (presumably distillation). Process synthesis principles will be needed to determine the optimal structure of the distillation train. A full material and energy balance of the process is required. Knowledge of chemical thermodynamics is necessary to write the material and energy balances correctly. A control scheme cannot be implemented without the balance equations. Finally, with all of this information in hand, an economic analysis can finally be performed to tell us whether the separation process is profitable. If the process is unprofitable, a new process needs to be synthesized. Competing process designs could prove to be more profitable, as sometimes chemical processing can be done in parallel (e.g. reactive distillation, reactive membrane separations, and catalytic distillation).

4.4 Computers and the Core Chemical Engineering Subjects

"Computers are like bikinis. They save people a lot of guesswork."

-Sam Ewing

This section could be a book unto itself, but I don't want to drown the reader in mathematical esoterica. The phenomena chemical engineers study are very complicated, and unlike the courses you have taken in high school, hand-written solutions are typically impossible. The exponential increase in computing power over the past decades has revolutionized data analysis, mathematical modeling, and design in the field [37]. As is typically the case in scientific revolutions, what was once a boon eventually becomes a necessity. Skillful computer use is mandatory for anyone interested in pursuing a career in the field.

One area where mathematics and computers intersect is in the area of process synthesis, where a team of chemical engineers try to come up with the best flowsheet they can to manufacture a given product.

Once the flowsheet is written, it is necessary to simulate the flowsheet on the computer to solve the material and energy balance equations, so that a proper economic analysis can be done. Calculations in optimization, flowsheeting, process control, and simulation which were previously laborious or impossible can now be done on a desktop computer. Typically on a process flowsheet, we have "extra" variables left over which we need to specify, but also directly impact the profitability of our process. This leads to the mathematical optimization step, where the computer is used to hunt through this set of "extra" variables for the most profitable settings for the plant. The sheer scale of the problems in process synthesis is staggering. Modeling and simulation of a chemical plant can involve over 200,000 variables, and optimization of chemical plants have been performed with over 500,000 decision variables [36]. The interested reader is directed to chapter 12 in the appendix for more information on optimization.

Computers are used elsewhere in process design as well. To exploit economies-of-scale, chemical engineers are frequently involved in the scale-up of chemical processes [40], [41]. It is one thing to synthesize a few milligrams of a substance using lab-scale equipment, but it is another matter entirely to profitably mass-produce it. Sophisticated mathematical and computer tools are often used to assist in the scale-up process, and scale-up ratios of 50,000 to 1 have been successfully executed using computer process models [36].

Transport phenomena studies the basic transport processes of mass transfer, momentum transfer, and heat transfer. The equations that govern these phenomena are, in general, coupled nonlinear partial differential equations, that are only solvable for very simple cases. The basic equations of fluid flow – which solve for the velocity field of the fluid – are the "continuity equation" and the "Navier-Stokes equations" [42]. These equations, for practical problems (e.g. for modeling the injection of gasoline into a car engine), require the use of powerful computers and specialized computer codes to obtain a fast solution. Problems become especially challenging when non-Newtonian fluids, heat transfer, and chemical reactions must also be modeled. The basic equations of mass, energy, and momentum transfer are only a subset of a more general set of equations termed "transport equations," or "conservation laws." Conservation laws also exist for more arcane quantities, such as entropy, number density, and neutron flux [43].

The controllability of chemical processes is also math and computer intensive. Ideally, we wish to design a control system that ensures worker safety, public health, and product quality. Once a dynamic model of a process has been written, it is possible to design a control scheme for it. Simulation of the process response to various disturbances is then analyzed using a computer. The behavior of the control scheme is investigated thoroughly on a computer for stability and potential safety impact before being implemented.

4.5 Overlap with Other Engineering Sub-Fields

"Great discoveries and improvements invariably involve the cooperation of many minds. I may be given credit for having blazed the trail, but when I look at the subsequent developments I feel the credit is due to others rather than to myself."

-Alexander Graham Bell

Since chemical engineering encompasses such a broad knowledge base, there is significant overlap between it and several other engineering fields. Some areas of significant overlap are:

1. Aerospace Engineering – Aerospace and chemical engineers both study control theory in great detail, as well as the thermodynamics of various engines used to power heavier-than-air craft. Chemical engineers have specialized knowledge that can enable them to model the burning of fuels in a jet or rocket engine.

2. Computer Science – This interaction is more a case of computer science know-how intruding into chemical engineering, rather than the other way around. Chemical engineers involved in process systems engineering are often tasked with solving extremely large mathematical problems – especially constrained optimization problems. Often these problems require a computer to solve them, but the real challenge lies in completely defining the problem mathematically, and constructing the algorithm for its solution. Important questions are, "How much memory does the solution require? How does the time required to solve the problem scale with the size of the problem?" Furthermore, problems involving the use of artificial intelligence and big data analytics are becoming more common in chemical engineering. Many industries – especially the pharmaceutical, retail,

healthcare, and petroleum industries, as well as the military – are swamped with data but lack ways of converting it into actionable knowledge [44]. Artificial intelligence is increasingly important to the operation of chemical plants, and also to the modeling of certain phenomena.

3. Materials Engineering – Chemical engineers bring a sophisticated knowledge of various materials to the table, especially plastics, polymers, composites, and biomaterials. Furthermore, chemical engineers have the special knowledge of process synthesis required for the economical mass production of a given new material. What good would Kevlar have done for the military and police forces if Kevlar could never be economically mass-manufactured?

4. Electrical and Computer Engineering – Electrical engineers and chemical engineers are both intimately familiar with control theory. Probably the biggest area of interaction lies in the mass production of semiconductors, microprocessor computer chips, hard drives, and other computer components whose manufacture is based on the precise manipulation of matter. Process systems engineering principles also have much application in the synthesis and optimization of electrical power systems, and also the design of electric power plants.

5. Mechanical – Probably the most significant regions of overlap between mechanical and chemical engineering are in the design of materials and thermodynamics. Mechanical engineers are always on the lookout for better materials, and ways to make better-performing engines. Chemical engineers possess the knowledge needed for the design of cheaper, stronger materials that mechanical engineers like. Chemical engineers also have knowledge of the sophisticated modeling methods needed to mathematically describe the operation of internal combustion engines and gas turbine engines.

Other fields possess some overlap as well, such as systems engineering, petroleum engineering, nuclear engineering, and various other materials engineering majors (e.g. metallurgical engineering).

4.6 What Chemical Engineers Don't Do During Their Education

"We know what we are, but know not what we may be."

-William Shakespeare

While the typical chemical engineering curriculum does involve laboratory courses, there is actually little hands-on work when in school. The experiments that are done in chemical engineering labs are often not very exciting either – usually just waiting for a pot to boil, a solution to change color, or a steel bar to heat fully. Expensive, fragile instrumentation (e.g. various spectroscopy tools, scanning electron microscopes, and transmission electron microscopes) is usually off-limits to undergraduates. There wasn't much hands-on work during my undergraduate education, there wasn't much opportunity to play with chemicals, and there was very little actual chemistry. There was virtually no biochemistry. However, when doing undergraduate research or in graduate school, there can be a significant hands-on component to your work. This is especially true if you study catalysis, biological systems, polymers, or any other materials-focused research.

There was however, far more computer usage than I expected. Many problems encountered in chemical engineering require the use of a computer. Some graduate students do their entire doctoral dissertation in a computational field. Some of my friends in graduate school never even bothered showing up to the building on very cold days. All they needed was their own computer to do their work, and they would just work remotely from home.

Furthermore, chemical engineers don't "plug and chug" equations. The degree is not about plugging in numbers you see on a page and plugging them into a formula – that task is only a few pegs above a trained ape's capability. Companies are not going to pay you $80,000 a year to plug-and-chug equations. Venture capitalists are not going to hook you up with money to plug-and-chug. The world just doesn't work that way. What is desired is people who can think.

5 Preparing for Chemical Engineering School

5.1 Am I Cut Out for Chemical Engineering?

"In all things success depends on previous preparation, and without such previous preparation there is sure to be failure."

-Confucius

If you enjoy mathematics, physics, and chemistry, then chemical engineering might be the path for you. But chemical engineering is not for dilettantes. You have to be very smart, and have a serious interest in pursuing study of its core subjects. I advise a minimum SAT score of 1200, with at least a 650 on the mathematics section if you are serious about chemical engineering – or engineering school in general. An SAT score of 1200 corresponds to an IQ of approximately 123, which is reasonably in the ballpark of a chemical engineer [45], [46]. I had a 1470 SAT score, and I found the undergraduate chemical engineering curriculum at USF to be extremely challenging.

Strong math skills are mandatory for having a fighting chance in engineering school, and getting an "A" in some low-level high school mathematics courses is not proof that you can handle a real college-level course load. If you are getting A's in difficult, high-level mathematics courses (e.g. AP Calculus), then that is a big plus.

Orderliness and organization are also strong skills to have. I understand that organization can be a difficult skill to master, and in high school the course load is generally not difficult enough to warrant a high-precision organization system. This is not the case in engineering school. Being orderly and organized in how you do your homework, store your notes and papers, and track your time usage is a powerful set of skills to have. Professors and teaching assistants quickly grow annoyed with messy work and deduct points accordingly. If you miss an exam due to time mismanagement, your professors aren't going to cut you any slack.

Your psychology and personality also impact your potential success in chemical engineering. Are you the kind of person who quits or gives up easily? Can you handle planning and executing projects that require a full semester to pull off? Can you handle sacrificing fun and frivolity in favor of studying? Do you have problems with drugs and alcohol? Can you work well with other people, in a team setting? Do you react to frustration with anger? Can you teach yourself new skills without anyone there to hold your hand?

5.2   The AP Program and Learning Calculus

"There are no secrets to success. It is the result of preparation, hard work, and learning from failure."

-Colin Powell

The AP program is an excellent way to prepare for college-level coursework. If you end up enjoying AP Chemistry, Calculus, and Physics, then chemical engineering might be right up your alley. The International Baccalaureate program is also a great way to prepare, though I know little about it because it was not offered at my high school when I attended.

In high school, your level of mathematics hits the ceiling at calculus. Should you have interest in becoming a chemical engineer, you should learn calculus backwards and forwards. Take Advanced Placement Calculus in high school, and pass the examination with a 4 or 5 (preferably a 5). If you cannot do this, you should think very hard before pursuing engineering school further. At the absolute minimum when you get to college, you should have completed a pre-calculus course, so that you will be ready-to-go for calculus in your first semester.

Preparation, though, should not stop when you get off the school bus. We live in an age of overwhelming information. Books on virtually any subject can be bought cheaply off Amazon. Google and Wikipedia make most of human knowledge accessible. Back in high school, I worked in my free time on learning differential equations and higher-level mathematics, in order to give myself a head-start when I got to engineering school. I found that strategy to be highly successful, and strongly recommend it. You could do the same with an advanced calculus textbook. If your goal is to be successful in chemical engineering, then I do not think it is possible to overdose on calculus. It is the basic language in which high-level science and mathematics is written.

As far as learning calculus on your own, I proffer a few suggestions. For a standard text on the topic, Silvanus Thompson's *Calculus Made Easy* was written with the self-starter in mind. Since the text is so old, it is in the public domain and available for free on Project Gutenberg [47]. A helpful study guide is *Calculus the Easy Way* by Douglas Downing [48]. For auditory learners, MIT has made available Herb Gross's old lectures from 1970, which thoroughly discuss the subject of single-variable calculus [49]. If you are a rather bright high school student, and can get through this calculus jazz without breaking a sweat, I recommend going a little further with Tennenbaum and Pollard's *Ordinary Differential Equations*. It's about $15 on Amazon [50]. A text on linear algebra would prove very useful as well.

The general strategy for self-learning is basically the same for any subject: watch the video lectures, read the book, take notes, review as necessary, do problems from the book until comfort is achieved, and "ask around" if you get stuck. "PhysicsForums" and "StackExchange" can be helpful places for getting help when stuck.

5.3 Learning Computer Programming in High School

"It's all talk until the code runs."

-Ward Cunningham

Another significant way to prepare in high school is to learn computer programming. This wasn't offered at my high school, but it is increasingly available. If your school offers a computer programming course, you should take it and ace it. Computers and programming expertise are indispensable to chemical engineering calculations, and knowing how to program will significantly reduce your work load during your study into the profession.

But which programming language to learn, when there are legions of them? As far as preparing for engineering school, I offer four suggestions:

- Microsoft Excel

- MATLAB

- GNU Octave

- Python

In addition to one of these other languages, Microsoft Excel is probably a software tool you should learn how to use. While I think Excel is inferior for scientific computing, it is very commonly used in industry. Knowing how to manipulate and compute quantities in Excel is an essential skill to have.

MATLAB (MATrix LABoratory) is a software programming environment geared towards the rapid prototyping of new software solutions. Much of the "book keeping" required from languages such as C and C++ is not necessary in MATLAB. The purpose of MATLAB is to quickly and efficiently solve complicated problems in science and engineering without requiring a great deal of programming finesse. MATLAB's big selling point is that it contains a huge variety of different solvers ready-to-go for different kinds of mathematical problems, provided you have the correct add-on packages installed. Root-finding, mathematical optimization, nonlinear regression, multiobjective optimization, solution of nonlinear algebraic equations, and other solvers are available. Another great feature is that MATLAB comes with an extensive set of tools for plotting and visualizing complicated data. MATLAB also has a fairly active user community on the MATLAB Central File Exchange, where thousands of code add-ons are available for free. Lastly, MATLAB has extensive help documentation available, making the tool relatively easy to learn. The main drawback to MATLAB is the price. While the price for a student license is reasonable ($99 as of this writing), a commercial license costs over $2,000, and the toolboxes cost about $1,000 a piece.

GNU Octave is a free alternative to MATLAB. The language is almost identical to MATLAB, and most programs that run with MATLAB will run with Octave – assuming specific MATLAB add-on packages are not required. The primary advantage over MATLAB is that Octave is 100% free to use. The drawbacks are that Octave does not have as many of the advanced solvers available as MATLAB does and the out-of-the-box plotting routines are inferior.

Lastly is Python. Unlike MATLAB and GNU Octave, Python is a

"real" programming language. As such, Python has significantly more capabilities than those tools. Python also has a very large, active user base, and many code packages are available for solving common science and engineering problems. Furthermore, the user-created add-on packages of NumPy, SciPy, and Matplotlib give Python almost the same capabilities that MATLAB has. Also, like Octave, Python is free to use. For self-teaching Python, the text by Lutz is comprehensive [51].

I would advise you to simply pick one of these options – in addition to Excel – and study it in detail. Apply it to your homework problems and projects in school. Learn what tools are available for Python if you go that route. Come up with your own problems and try solving them. This is invaluable experience that will make your life immensely easier in engineering school.

5.4 Handling Scientific Units

"If you cannot measure it, you cannot improve it."

-Lord Kelvin

As an engineering student, you will be dealing with scientific units a lot. I cannot overemphasize this point. If you have trouble with converting units, you are going to have a very difficult time in engineering school and in the work place. My work in graduate school required very close attention to scientific units. If your units are not working out correctly, it is automatic proof that your work is wrong. A submitted journal article with unit errors in the manuscript will almost certainly be rejected.

As my undergraduate thermodynamics professor, Dr. Smith, would say: "Units will make your lunch. Units will eat your lunch." I became very comfortable with using the proper engineering units in his class, and always had to make sure my units all canceled out properly. While I do love America, I think that the Imperial system of measurement is utterly inferior to the SI system, and wish we would abrogate the Imperial system and adopt SI instead. Alas, this is unlikely to ever happen in my lifetime. If the reader ever takes an engineering thermodynamics course, I am certain they will understand just how cumbersome the Imperial system is. Perhaps my complaints are unjustified though – we did after all, put a man on the moon using Imperial engineering units.

During my time at my job, I've had to do some pretty tricky unit conversions. If I had to ask my boss how to do this basic task, things would probably have gotten very ugly, very fast. I strongly advise you practice this skill until you have it down pat. I've been in college for eleven years, and I still use the same factor-label method I learned in AP Chemistry in the eleventh grade back in 2003 [52]. I advise you, during your time in high school physics and chemistry classes, to practice converting units until you are blue in the face. It will only make things easier down the road.

5.5 Earning Scholarship Money

"Education costs money, but then so does ignorance."

-Claus Moser

You should avail yourself to get as much scholarship and financial aid money as possible to keep your student loan balance as low as possible. As I discussed in section 3.6, the worth of any degree declines with increased borrowing and longer time-to-graduation. If you have to spend yourself into the grave to get your degree, financially you're better off working minimum wage.

With my test scores, grades, and volunteering efforts, I qualified for Florida's Bright Futures[13] scholarship, which completely paid the tuition costs for my undergraduate studies. Had I attended an out-of-state school, I would have gone tens of thousands of dollars into debt. I consider myself extremely fortunate – my tuition and much of my books were covered with my scholarship, and my mother had saved up plenty of money to pay for my room and board on campus. After all was said and done, my student loan balance after eleven years of school

---

[13] The Bright Futures program presents a humorous paradox. The program is funded by the Florida Lottery. Lotteries, however, are overwhelmingly played by impoverished people who don't know how math, probability, or investments work. Instead of aiding upward social mobility, the program is essentially a huge wealth transfer from the poor to the middle class and government. But hey, I'm not above taking free money.

was about $25,000. While that might sound like a lot of money, it is a pittance compared to the amount of education I received and the worth of the degrees. I've already got about two-thirds of it paid off.

5.6 Learning How to Act and Speak to People Properly

"Be polite; write diplomatically; even in a declaration of war one observes the rules of politeness."

-Otto von Bismarck

During my brief time on this planet, I have observed a pronounced decline in basic courtesy that ought to be extended to strangers. Instead of asking a stranger a direct question, first say, "Excuse me", or "Pardon me." When addressing adults, schoolteachers, professors, and teaching assistants, use "Sir" and "Ma'am." Hold the door for other people, not just ladies. Take your hat off when in a building. Dress respectably; don't wear marijuana-leaf t-shirts to class and expect to be taken seriously. Avoid the use of foul language in public. Bathe regularly, and use deodorant. Brush and floss your teeth every day to avoid dragon breath. Instead of sleeping in class at college, just skip class and go take a nap at home. These basic, common courtesies have nothing to do with your academics, but they go a long way to being considered someone who "has their stuff together."

5.7 The Top Chemical Engineering Programs

"Accept the challenges so that you can feel the exhilaration of victory."

-General George S. Patton

The top chemical engineering programs according to *U.S. News and World Report* (as of this writing) are:

1. MIT
2. UC Berkeley
3. Stanford
4. University of Texas – Austin
5. University of Minnesota – Twin Cities

6. Georgia Tech
7. University of Wisconsin – Madison
8. CalTech
9. Princeton
10. University of Delaware
11. University of Michigan – Ann Arbor
12. Purdue University

I am skeptical of the worth of the education at top universities. I attended undergraduate chemical engineering at the University of South Florida, a school which – at least when I attended – was unranked as far as chemical engineering was concerned. However, in retrospect I feel that I received an excellent education at USF and met a lot of intelligent people. From what I have heard from alumni at highly-ranked schools, the education, to be blunt, sucks. The professors are mega big-shots devoted to research and don't necessarily care much for your education – they don't have to. I outright asked a girl who went to Cornell if the money was worth it to go to there for undergraduate chemical engineering. Her answer? "Nope!" Another professor I spoke to did his undergraduate at a top-ranked university, and said the professors there did not give a rat's behind about the undergraduates' education. Lastly, a professor I spoke to during doctoral recruiting said her own school was probably not worth it for undergraduate chemical engineering studies due to the enormous expense, and that a state school was probably more appropriate for a person of modest means.

Another problem with top universities is that their programs are usually very large, meaning that your class sizes will be huge. At USF, my classes in the chemical engineering program were about twenty-five to forty students. At Purdue however, classes could have over 150 people in them. This makes it hard to distinguish yourself, making it difficult to secure recommendations for graduate school or employment. Also, large class sizes reduce the amount of attention a professor is capable of spending on you personally, meaning more of the coursework will be up to you to learn by yourself.

However, if you have the stats necessary to get into a top school, you should probably apply. If you get in, see what kind of financial assistance is being offered by the school, and if the debt load is manageable. The best programs have enormous name recognition, and top companies hire aggressively from these schools. Such companies also aggressively fund departments whose graduates have paid off for a company's bottom line [29]. I am just making it clear that if you go into such a program, you will probably be on your own. The professors probably will not care about you, and the teaching assistants will probably have better things to do than hold your hand.

Probably the biggest plus to the top programs has nothing to do with the professors or the university's facilities. The biggest plus is that you will be spending four years in close proximity to some extraordinarily bright people, most of whom have over 1500 SAT scores, who can make for powerful connections in your career at school and in the business world. You will also get a better education as well – but perhaps not in the way you think. Of course I learned a great deal from my professors in school, but I learned a ton of useful skills and tricks from my fellow classmates. Your professors do not have the time or inclination to work with you for several days through a project, but your fellow classmates certainly will work with you. After all, you're taking the same class! Furthermore, if you have entrepreneurial interests, the top schools (e.g. Stanford University) have gone to great lengths to foster a spirit of entrepreneurship into their programs. If you have the ambition of Lucifer in you, and desire "wealth beyond the dreams of avarice," then getting involved with entrepreneur-minded people in the chemical engineering department is probably a smart move. We'll discuss that in greater depth in chapter .

5.8 Quality of Life at University

"Winter is coming."

-George R.R. Martin, *A Game of Thrones*

There are quality-of-life issues that should be considered as well should you choose to go far away to college. When I attended USF, my mother was only an hour's drive away, and she would visit me frequently during the weekends. That really helped me stay sane during my undergraduate years. Had I gone to a far away school, I think I would have missed my mom too much.

USF was warm all year-round, while some of the schools I listed above become bleak, frozen wastelands in the winter time. Purdue University becomes a miserable icebox for five months out of the year.

If cold weather is a problem for you, consider attending a school further south.

Crime is also a problem at some universities, even top-ranked ones. While the campus may be safe, there are colleges for which the surrounding area is a demilitarized zone. Marquette University here in Milwaukee has this problem. Before applying to a certain school, I would look up crime statistics for the surrounding area, as well as annual crime reports for the university at large. It makes little sense to work so hard to get into a top-program, just to die in a "robbery gone wrong" a few weeks before graduation.

5.9   The Importance of Accreditation in Engineering School

"Students are not greater than their teacher. But the student who is fully trained will become like the teacher."

-The New Testament, Luke 6:40

Accreditation is what makes your engineering degree worth more than the paper it is printed on. When a school's engineering program is "accredited," it means an independent third-party organization has inspected the school's facilities, faculty, and curricula, and agree that they measure up to a minimum standard of quality. The main body that handles the accreditation of engineering programs in the United States is the Accreditation Board for Engineering and Technology (ABET).

The accreditation process requires routine inspections. ABET personnel physically come to the campus and review the various facilities. Laboratories are checked that the equipment can actually serve the educational role the school's curriculum says it can. They also check for adherence to proper safety protocols. ABET also accredits online-only engineering schools, but I would be wary about the quality of these programs, and cannot vouch for how much clout they hold with employers.

The American Institute of Chemical Engineers provides a full list of ABET-accredited chemical engineering programs, and the ABET website has a comprehensive search feature [53], [54]. Before enrolling in any engineering program, you should check that it is ABET-accredited. If it isn't, you should avoid it like a mattress full of bedbugs. For-profit colleges are notorious for offering non-accredited technology programs, which do not have any pull with employers. Many states will not allow you to sit for a professional engineering examination if your school was not ABET-accredited.

6 Succeeding in Chemical Engineering School

6.1 The Necessity of Determination and Frequent Study

"Energy and persistence conquer all things."

-Benjamin Franklin

Engineering school is tough. You need to be a determined, hard worker to succeed in undergraduate engineering, and there is significant effort made by the faculty to "weed out" people who are not capable of handling the demanding coursework and subject matter. Washout rates are often around 50%, depending on the school – and those were students who did well in high school and thought they were capable of doing engineering. Unless you attended an elite preparatory school, or aced your courses in the AP program, it is unlikely your high school education has prepared you for a rigorous course of study in chemical engineering. Exams are exceptionally difficult in engineering school, and waiting until the day before to start studying is a guaranteed way to flunk out.

Daily study – with perhaps a break every few days – is one of the most important habits you can develop for yourself in college. There are all sorts of study methods, but ultimately none of these methods work if you don't actually do them. Studying is a multi-step process, and it takes a long time to do effectively. Don't be one of those whiners who complains "I don't get this stuff," but upon questioning reveals they have not even done the required reading. Read your books. Take written notes, and organize them appropriately. A good sign that you are studying effectively is that you will eventually be able to write concrete, direct questions about the things you don't understand. These questions can then be brought up in class, during the teaching assistant's office hours, or during the professor's office hours.

Drawing on my own experiences as an undergraduate at the University of South Florida, I will put things in perspective. In my first few years of attendance, the USF Library was open until 2 AM. I would finish up classes at around 4 PM for the day, eat dinner, and then head directly to the library and work on my homework and study for my courses, all the way to 1:45 AM when the library staff would kick us out – with perhaps a break in there somewhere for more food at the nearby Subway in Cooper Hall. That might sound unreasonable, but that is what it took to succeed. The big problem is that you have no choice but to study everything at once. Your professors will each chop the semester into thirds or fourths, and schedule their exams accordingly. This means all of your exams come at the same time, like an artillery barrage or a hurricane. If you want to succeed in engineering school, you will need to study several hours a day for your courses.

Paradoxically, I did not study much the evening before exams. I would study a little, but not with the same intensity as I would during the calm periods. It is too late to study for an exam the night before, and for me it only created stress and self-doubt. To paraphrase Sun Tzu, the battle is won well before the battle actually begins. A pro-athlete doesn't simply show up on the field and win, as if it were a chance occurrence like the weather. Who spent more time in the gym? Who trained harder? Which army was better prepared? Preparing the night before a major exam is a guaranteed way to see your army slaughtered. Study diligently and daily out of personal habit, and you will see your army crush the opposition.

6.2 The Dread Specter of Temptation

"Let the future tell the truth, and evaluate each one according to his work and accomplishments. The present is theirs; the future, for which I have really worked, is mine."

-Nikola Tesla

A further impediment to succeeding in engineering school is the enormous amount of temptation and vice prevalent at universities. When I was a freshman at USF (fall 2004 to spring 2005), the fashionable thing to do was play video games excessively, smoke weed, get drunk, and fornicate. I rejected this foolishness and focused on studying. If you're serious about your schooling, you need to be able to say "No!" to things that are only going to get in the way of getting what you want – and that includes alcohol, staying up late, video games, love interests, drugs, and partying.

That's not to say you won't be able to have fun, but it does mean you will need to be responsible with your time. People pursuing easier majors will be able to fill their days with fun activities, and then attend some classes on the side. With you, you'll be filling your day with classes and studying, with some fun activities on the side.

6.3 The Temptations of the Flesh and Their Consequences

"Unzip your pants and your brains fall out."

-My Great-Aunt Helen

You'll also have to tolerate seeing your friends and roommates having lots of fun while you are spending a great deal of your time studying. Heck, I remember one time in my junior year of college, my neighbor brought some girl home late at night, and shut the door. I had to hear her moan, giggle, and squeal all throughout the night through the thin walls while I had to study for an exam the next day. As a red-blooded young man, these are the sorts of trials that can make one seriously question their commitment and dedication to a cause, and wonder if it's really all worth it.

For the young men reading this, women are especially problematic, since if one gets pregnant, you're in a lot of trouble. As radio personality Tom Leykis has said, "Every sperm is a little credit card – and it has to be controlled." It is virtually impossible to handle engineering school when you have to also work to make child support payments. While I knew several married couples that had children in engineering school, I know of only one fellow who got a girl pregnant outside of marriage, and still managed to get his bachelor's degree in engineering. It took him eight years to get it instead of four. The situation is not any better if you are a girl who gets pregnant in school, who must now deal with going to class and also raising a child on top of it. In summary, if partying doing drugs, getting wasted, and getting laid is your goal in university, then engineering school is not for you.

As an undergraduate, I went on a grand total of two dates during all of engineering school. This was not for lack of interest, but simply due to there being only twenty-four hours in a day. Eventually, I just accepted that engineering school is not the place for dating; it's the place for building a future for yourself. If you can manage it time wise, go for it. It certainly can be done, as many friends of mine had girl-friends in school. However, I personally did not want to spend time on a woman when there was simply too much studying and work to do. Furthermore, I did not have a car or much money, so there was little to offer a woman other than my charming personality. Get it through your skull – you are there at engineering school to study, not chase skirts or boys.

On the subject of studying and young ladies, the USF Library was often flooded with them. This made studying extraordinarily difficult to do on the first floor, as their beauty was so distracting. I strongly doubt you (if you are a young man) will be able to focus on your work when there are hordes of beautiful twenty-something college women running around in tight tops and mini-skirts. You need to get away from that during study time. Study in isolated regions (e.g the basement) of the library, far away from gaze or earshot of these women. Keep your eyes on the prize!

6.4 Managing Your Friendships and Ensuring Their Value

"Keep away from people who try to belittle your ambitions. Small people always do that, but the really great make you feel that you, too, can become great."

-Mark Twain

Saying "No!" will also need to extend to your social circles and friendships. There are a lot of screwed-up people at college, especially in your first two years of school. Periodically, you will need to put on the cold, hard demeanor of an accountant, and take an inventory of the people in your life. Some people are genuine friends and are deserving of the label "asset." Toxic, negative, gloomy, dysfunctional people are liabilities. Liabilities go on the left side of the ledger, assets go on the right. At the end of the day, all accounts need to be settled, and that means crossing off the liabilities on the ledger sheet.

I've had to do this several times, when someone who I once thought was cool eventually revealed themselves to just be a stumbling block to my goal of becoming a chemical engineer. Avoid people who doubt your capabilities and encourage you to give up and take an easier route like theirs. You have to cross these people out of your life and move on. We always have people in our life we wish we could help, but your job in college is not to be Albert Schweitzer or Mother Teresa. Your goal is to get that degree you came for.

6.5 Land of the Lotus-Eaters

"A junkie spends half his life waiting."

-William S. Burroughs

One particular strain of human liability is so common it requires special attention. I strongly urge the reader to avoid associating with abusers of drugs and alcohol when at college. An apt epithet I prefer to use when describing these people is "lotus-eaters," from the Greek epic poem *The Odyssey*. In the poem, Odysseus and his men land on a mysterious isle where lotuses bloom. Some of Odysseus's men eat the lotus fruit, become intoxicated, and want to abandon their efforts at returning to their homeland of Ithaca.

Lotus-eaters do not dwell in the real world or think their thoughts in concrete terms. They let drugs do their thinking for them. You are better than that, and you absolutely do not have time to listen to their baloney or hear about their self-inflicted problems. You're not doing yourself any good by being friends with lotus eaters, and are just setting yourself up to get nabbed by the cops. They are making a mess of their own lives, and they'll make a mess of yours too if you let them. I know of two chemical engineering students who routinely did drugs in college and were successful. Everyone else I met in college that was doing drugs was a nowhere-bound loser. They would bounce from major to major, incur tons of student debt, and eventually drop out of college, returning home as a great big nothing.

Alcohol is an especially big problem at universities, and is the source of much human misery. Around halfway through my graduate studies, I began noticing that many of my friends in the program had an unhealthy appetite for alcohol. While I enjoyed the sober company of my colleagues in the graduate program, I couldn't help but feel alienated and persistently like an outsider among the group because I didn't drink. It was fun to get together in the local parks for a picnic, play laser tag, play video games, or any other number of activities that didn't involve alcohol. But these activities were not in great supply, and most of the activities planned by the graduate students always, in some form, involved alcohol consumption. Many of my friends in the program were true connoisseurs of craft beer, and would routinely go to the smoke-filled pubs in Lafayette to drink themselves silly – and hopefully entice some local strumpet into bed.

I didn't like any of it. I had enough problems with loneliness and depression in graduate school, and did not want to compound them with alcohol, no matter how much more it would have let me fit into the group. For most of my five years at Purdue, this was a constant problem. Some of my colleagues became alcoholics. Beer pong was hugely popular, though I just viewed it as another stupid drinking game that was, by its own construction, a race to the bottom. There was just too much drinking, and I failed to see any value in any of it. It's an expensive habit that ruins your health and sets you up for all kinds of legal trouble. Some might laugh at my Magic the Gathering habit, but I can always sell my Magic cards and get most of my money back. Those thousands of dollars my colleagues wasted on Jack Daniels, Wild Turkey, Jaegermeister, and overpriced craft beer for five years? It was all flushed down the urinals of the bars and pubs in Lafayette, Indiana, and they'll never get it back.

To minimize these problems, I advise getting into some type of honors or sobriety dormitory during your freshman year of college. Honors dorms typically – though not always – contain students who are more dedicated to their studying. Sobriety dorms openly ban alcohol and drugs, and people who violate that policy get kicked out. Hindsight is 20/20, but if I could do my freshman year over again, I would have enrolled into the honors dorm at USF and saved myself a great deal of headache.

6.6 Avoiding Dysfunctional Study Groups and Solitary Study

"The thoughtful soul to solitude retires."

-Omar Khayyam

This advice is probably counter-intuitive, and also flies in the face of much conventional wisdom, but I think I am in the right: except under limited circumstances, avoid study groups in engineering school. Your own professors will likely encourage you to "work together on problems," and "put your heads together." This is malarkey. In my own experience, study groups are a huge waste of time, and do not lead to better understanding of the material compared to studying in solitude.

There are several reasons for this, but the main underlying reason is the simple fact that most people are not going to be as committed to studying as you are. Here is an example dialogue of how a study group tends to go:

"Hi, Joe, I was able to get problems one and three, but had trouble on two. Were you able to get problem number two?"

"Oh, I haven't done the reading yet, Mark. I was going to read it during the study session."

"Umm... okay. How about you, Suzy? Were you able to get problem two?"

Suzy is distracted texting her latest boyfriend on her phone, has cat videos up on her laptop, and doesn't respond.

"Oh good grief. How about you, Rob? Were you able to get problem two?"

"Uhhh, I couldn't get problem one. Could you help me with it, Mark?"

"I give up!"

There are many things wrong with the way this study group is operating. Joe has not even done the required reading, and for some likely-ridiculous reason, wants to read in the presence of his study group members. Suzy is taking up space and precious oxygen, has the attention span of a hummingbird, and should not have been invited to participate. While Rob at least made some effort to participate, he still did not attempt all of the problems. Now Mark needs to serve as Rob's tutor, and he isn't getting paid for it. Mark is clearly putting more effort into the group but isn't getting anything out of it for himself. He would be better off using the time he spends getting Rob up to speed studying by himself – and he would be far better off not having to deal with morons like Joe and Suzy.

The only time you should agree to participate in a study group is when the following ground rules are in place before agreeing to meet with people and permitting them to make demands on your time:

1. Everyone must do the required reading before the meeting. This is non-negotiable.

2. Everyone must have attended class and taken the notes, or if absent, gotten the notes from someone else afterwards.

3. Everyone must have made a "good faith" effort to attempt all of the homework problems.

4. All electronic devices are to be put away while studying, unless looking up relevant information on Wikipedia or Google. Texting is not permitted during the study session.

If you can find a small cadre of intelligent people who will agree and abide to these rules, a study group may be helpful in learning the material. If someone shows up to the meeting with a baloney excuse for not accomplishing rules 1 through 3, or starts texting and looking at cat videos on their phone in violation of rule 4, gather your belongings, get up, and walk away. It's just not worth wasting your time with people who are not serious about studying at the same level you are.

Solitary study, with or without music, is the best way to get things done in engineering school. Simply get your books and papers, head to a secluded, quiet section of the library, bring your MP3 player or phone, sit down, turn on the music, and start reading, studying, taking notes, and working problems. There really is no secret to learning. The real "secret" is that the people searching for the "secret" are lazy and don't want to do their work. If you want to succeed in engineering school, and want to perform at a high level, you must discipline your mind to study for long hours in solitude. If you run into a problem you cannot solve immediately – which is guaranteed to be the case in engineering school – try to attack the problem from many different angles. Do not immediately search for the answer when you are confronted with a tough problem. Let it stew for a day or two. You'd be surprised how clever you can be when you dwell on a problem for a good long while.

As a caution however, I advise the reader to get up, stretch, and walk around for five minutes every two hours. Sitting for long periods of time is dangerous, and can lead to a stroke, a pulmonary embolism, or deep vein thrombosis. Sitting and studying for four or more consecutive hours is a recipe for disaster in the long run. Get up and move around during your study breaks!

6.7 Controlling Your Video Game Play Time

"Video games are a waste of time for men with nothing else to do. Real brains don't do that."

-Ray Bradbury

Alright, I admit Mr. Bradbury is being a little rough here on video games, but he's got a point. I used to be a huge video gamer[14] . I loved playing *Warcraft II* and *Command and Conquer* when I was in elementary school. All of Blizzard Entertainment's old titles, such as *Diablo* and *Starcraft*, occupied much of my time in middle school. I was a full-blown addict to *Diablo 2* in the first half of high school. I actually used to want to make video games, and even considered going to college for video game design – a decision that I would have deeply regretted. I could write several paragraphs listing all of the video games I used to play and extracted much joy from. But video games are a major dead-end. They consume an enormous amount of time and money, and at the end of the day you get nothing for it. There is no payoff. Zero. Zip. Zilch. The best advice I can give to someone interested in engineering school is to get your play time under control. Instead of playing video games excessively, occupy your time productively, such as going to the gym, going for a run, spending time with friends, starting a side business, or studying. These are activities that have a chance of paying off. With video games, your expected payoff is always the same: zero. That being said, it is okay to play video games, as long as you do not let your play time interfere with your studies.

I strongly recommend against playing online role-playing games, as these games not only cost money, but are intentionally designed to be addictive so that you will continue to shell out the monthly subscription fee. Game companies have hired people with PhDs in behavioral psychology to research ways to make these games as addictive as possible [55]. Online role-playing games are like an electronic casino, only

---

[14] As Apostle Paul said of sinners, "...among whom I am the worst." (1 Timothy 1:15)

you're betting your time and money for worthless in-game objects.

I know of several people who screwed up their academic careers over video games. A guy I knew my first semester started off in chemical engineering at USF, but he blew off his exams in the second semester so he could go on raids in *World of Warcraft*[15] . He later switched to political science. One young man, "Frederick," I recall from the Honors dorm at USF my second year, was studying physics, but he absolutely could not kick his addiction to *World of Warcraft*. He eventually disappeared. Then in the fall of 2009, I went with another graduate student to the Muvico Hollywood 20 movie theater in Tampa, and well, well, well – guess who took our tickets? Frederick. He'd dropped out of school and abandoned his goal of being a physicist to become a ticket-taker at the movie theater, all because of *World of Warcraft*. There were also people back in Spring Hill who were hopelessly addicted to *World of Warcraft*. Instead of pursuing education or job training, they would work menial jobs to pay the electric bills and rent, and devote all of their spare time to playing *WoW*.

I wondered what was going to happen to these people in ten years when they realized they had been wasting their life playing that stupid video game. It's been ten years since I first had that thought. Now I have a doctorate and a great job. Several of my friends have gotten married. Some have entire families now, with children. A few of my friends have bought houses, or had them built. Some of my friends have passed the professional engineer's exam and are now fully-licensed professional engineers. What do these guys that wasted their twenties playing video games have to show for all of their time investment?

Nothing! Absolutely nothing!

6.8   Time Management in Engineering School

"So little done, so much to do."

-Cecil John Rhodes, last words

If you're not staying busy in engineering school, you're doing it wrong. Whether in undergraduate years or graduate school, you will be

---

[15] Or as I prefer to call it, "World of Warcrack."

busy as hell. Definitely get yourself a smartphone. Most people get smartphones simply so they can waste time on them playing video games, killing brain cells on social media, watching cat videos, and jamming to music. Nonetheless, they are useful tools for busy people. I held off on buying one until two years into graduate school, and I regret it. They are an invaluable tool for remembering where you need to be and when, having easy access to the internet and your email box, or taking down quick notes.

I am skeptical as to the worth of so-called "time management" systems. I never used such a system in school, and I did just fine. I think most time-management issues can be solved using calendar software hooked up to a smartphone. The Brad Ridder Time Management System was "Work like hell as soon as the assignment is given, and then have fun after it is finished." Of course my system isn't for everyone. Maybe you like more structure than that. If you are the kind of person who takes on lots of responsibilities, such as sports, student government, or clubs, then some kind of time management system might be a wise idea.

Most of what you read in time management books will probably not apply to your situation, or will be baloney. A semi-decent book I read was David Allen's *Getting Things Done* [56]. However, Mr. Allen recommends "delegating" tasks you don't want to do to other people, an option you do not have most of the time in school. I did, however, find Mr. Allen's folder-and-filing-cabinet system very useful in graduate school, especially as a teaching assistant. Ultimately, though, I feel the target audience for these types of books are simply lazy people looking "for an easy way out" of doing hard work. To make time-management systems function properly, you simply have to be self-disciplined enough to work on tasks you don't want to work on at a certain time.

Another important topic related to time management is your social media usage. Personally, I recommend against using social media (e.g. Facebook, Twitter, Instagram) when pursuing a demanding degree such as chemical engineering. Social media is generally a wasteland that does little to elevate one's consciousness or ability to think. It is also an enormous time sink. One can literally spend an entire day doing nothing but posting tripe on social media, only to look up and remember they had an exam they needed to study for. Furthermore, major companies always do a social media scan before they hire anyone, and unless your social media accounts are completely private, the company will look for reasons to exclude you from hiring consideration. One

58

photograph of you doing something foolish or illegal can cost you a good job, or land you in hot water with the cops. There is absolutely no reason to expose yourself in this manner. Play your cards close to the chest. Do yourself a huge favor, and pull the plug on social media.

6.9 Useful Technology for Chemical Engineering Students

"One machine can do the work of fifty ordinary men. No machine can do the work of one extraordinary man."

-Elbert Hubbard

Besides the aforementioned smartphone, get yourself a laptop computer for college. I never bothered with a desktop computer since I knew I would be moving frequently and didn't want to risk it getting destroyed. Laptops are much more amenable to being moved around than desktops. There are other devices too that can function as a computer replacement, such as a tablet. I have no experience with such devices – and don't want to spend the money on them – but they were quite popular among students at Purdue.

Calculators are a tricky subject, since what is permitted varies from school-to-school, and may have changed since I was an undergraduate. Throughout high school and college I used my brother's hand-me-down Texas Instruments TI-83 graphing calculator. It had a black and white display, and was somewhat slow, but it served me well until I lost it in 2012. Nowadays, graphing calculators come with all sorts of fancy color displays, but I'm not knowledgeable on actual performance increases that have been made over the past decade. Nonetheless, you will need a graphing calculator, and will need to learn how to use it. I learned virtually every function of the TI-83 over the course of engineering school, though I never bothered learning how to program with it. Whichever calculator you decide upon, practice, practice, practice with it until it becomes an extension of your body and mind.

Dropbox is an extremely useful service. I recommend undergraduate and graduate students obtain a Dropbox account for storing all of their files. Dropbox – as of this writing – is a manageable $99 a year for 1 terabyte of cloud storage. Set up a folder for each class and drop all of the course files into the corresponding folder. Scan all of your homework – no matter how poor your grade was – and upload it onto your Dropbox. If you make a formula sheet for an exam, scan that in as well. Scan in all of your tests and quizzes. With such an enormous amount of storage space available, you won't lose anything. All course documents that the professor makes freely available should also be downloaded. In this manner, after four years of college, the entirety of your education will be accessible to you. This will be a godsend when you get a job, and need to refer back to your old notes and homework in order to see how you solved a particular problem. As a handy bonus, Dropbox makes your files easily accessible from any device, and easy to share with anyone. As a graduate student, this can be a huge boon, if after a few years some confused graduate student from another university decides to email you asking you questions about your paper(s). If your code files and raw data sets are stored on the hard drive at your old alma mater, you won't be very helpful.

Another service which is extremely useful is Evernote [57]. Evernote is a note-taking program which has the very powerful feature of syncing across all of your devices (e.g. your phone, your laptop and your desktop computer). You can write yourself notes, embed graphics, and embed PDF files in your notes. Additionally, you can tag your notes as well for rapid searching and easy categorizing. Using Evernote, it is impossible to ever lose a thought again, as long as you have your smartphone on you. I am not too sure how useful Evernote will be for the undergraduate student, since Evernote came out when I was finished with classes, but it looks promising. Evernote however, looks incredibly powerful for graduate students involved in research, and I wish I had it when I was doing my PhD. All of your research work, such as graphics, figures, and raw data sets can be easily stored using Evernote, tagged appropriately, and automatically have the time and date logged. It is also reasonably priced: Evernote, as of this writing, costs $25 a year for most of the functionality. I personally have been using the free version to help me write this book, as I have not yet had a reason to upgrade to the "Plus" version. However, as a doctoral student at Purdue, I would have bought the Plus version without even blinking an eye.

Zotero is a free-to-use citation manager that makes it easy to keep track of the sources you are using when writing research papers or lab reports [58]. To use Zotero, download the add-on for your browser, and the correct plug-in for your word processing program (e.g. Microsoft Word or OpenOffice). Using your web browser, you can keep track of all your sources, whether they are books, YouTube videos, websites, journal articles, or government white papers. When you want to insert a citation, use the Zotero plug-in options in your word processor. If you rearrange your writing afterwards, Zotero will automatically renumber all of the sources for you. For a little extra money, Zotero offers cloud storage services for all of your source files.

Another extremely useful service I recommend is LastPass [59]. LastPass is a password management service, which stores all your web passwords. As an engineering student, you have far more important things to worry about than remembering passwords. Do not use the same password for everything, since this makes you vulnerable to a system breach and having your personal information stolen. LastPass has the powerful ability to generate long, random passwords for you, essentially making them impossible to hack. Some of my passwords are over a hundred characters long. LastPass can also store "secure notes," making it easy to store non-website passwords and locker combinations. The only catch is that you need to create a powerful master password to open your "vault" with. Obviously, you cannot forget your master password.

6.10 Being Orderly and Organized in Doing Homework and Taking Notes

"Education is what remains after one has forgotten what one has learned in school."

-Albert Einstein

To get the most out of your homework, write legibly. Do your homework on nice engineering paper, written in dark pencil. The most expedient way to do your homework is to do it "twice" – do the raw scratch-work on throw-away paper and then transcribe the complete solution onto nice engineering paper. When drawing diagrams, use a ruler, stencils, and French curves. Write out your logic in complete sentences for doing certain things. Refer to specific equations and pages in your textbook(s). This will not only greatly increase your understanding of the course material in preparation for the exams, but it will be a huge boon to you when you get a job and need to refer back to your old homework for guidance. You will not remember five or six years later what your logic was behind writing the equations down on the page.

Likewise with your note-taking, be as orderly as possible. Instead of taking notes in pencil, consider getting one of those multicolored ink pens that let you switch between different colors of ink. Don't write down just what the professor writes on the board; also write down useful things he says as well – though don't try to be a courtroom stenographer. If you ask a question, write down your question and what the professor's answer was. Likewise with your classmates' questions that prove insightful.

I have no experience with electronic note-taking using a tablet, but I have seen many students use this. I am skeptical as to the worth of such a system, but if it works for you, and you have the money to blow on an electronic tablet, then so be it. There are some benefits to going paperless – such as less stuff to move around, and less chance stuff will get lost. A drawback, though, to many computerized note-taking systems is the poor support for mathematical formulas, which dominates the education of engineers. Some systems, however, allow for direct drawing of notes onto the computer screen. Again, I am not sure of the efficacy of such a system, but it could be worth trying out. It just seems more straightforward to use pencil and paper.

If you decide to go the route of taking paper notes, make sure you have a binder for each class. Don't be foolish and throw your notes out after a class is done. You'll need them later in your career. Over the years, you'll probably accumulate a small army of three-ring binders holding all of your notes. This can be bothersome to lug around everywhere, but it is far better than throwing them out. This also goes for your textbooks. Do not sell your engineering textbooks! You will need them again at your job!

6.11 Keeping Your Computer Files Organized

"If anything can go wrong, it will."

-Murphy's Law

I used to not put much effort into organizing my computer files. I've had hard drives crash on me in the past, and as a result did not see much purpose in organizing my files. However, to reiterate the usefulness of Dropbox – or whatever cloud storage service you choose – you should put more effort than I did into organizing your computer files.

Since the storage is permanent, and the risk of data loss is virtually zero, it pays to put effort into organizing your files. This becomes extremely important should you go to graduate school, as you will constantly be dealing with large numbers of different files. You may think you'll be able to remember six months from now where you put something, but trust me, you won't. You'll need to have a good organizational structure for your computer files to ensure you can find files at a moment's notice. You might have prepared a complete manuscript only to be told by your adviser, "I don't like the way this figure is plotted. Try it from a different angle." Will you be able to find the specific data for that figure, from six months ago? Without a well-organized file system, you don't have a chance.

6.12 Keeping a Laboratory Notebook and Consistent Writing

"A tidy laboratory means a lazy chemist."

-Jöns Jacob Berzelius

This section mainly pertains to students doing research in chemical engineering. While it would be nice to keep an orderly laboratory notebook, the nature of research often makes this impossible, resulting in needless obsession. I tried many times to maintain what I felt was an "orderly" notebook, just to wind up feeling frustrated and inadequate. Nonetheless, try to keep the most orderly laboratory notebook you possibly can. Label and date every page. I recommend splurging on a premium bound notebook that already has the pages numbered. I found it very helpful to write down specific file names I worked with on a given day, making it easy to refer back to that work a week or two later. Always date every page. I recommend keeping each page specific only to a given date. If one page winds up being half-full, don't worry about filling in that blank – just continue on to the next.

Your laboratory notebook will probably end up becoming very messy, no matter how much effort you put into keeping it orderly. Part of your job as a graduate student or undergraduate researcher in engineering is to create order out of chaos. How do you logically reassemble this "blob" of notes, graphs, charts, and data into a coherent research communication?

As a doctoral student, I found periodic writing of my thoughts to be extremely useful, and this greatly hastened the completion of my dissertation. At least once a week, though feel free to write more often than this if you please, write down your thoughts on the literature you've read that week, and the experiments you've conducted. If you find this to be too herculean a task, then split the write-up into two or three sessions throughout the week. Doing this, you can quickly compile a vast body of research work that can easily be converted into published papers, and eventually a finished dissertation.

6.13 The Importance of Checking Your Work and Answering the Actual Question

"What the ancients called a clever fighter is one who not only wins, but excels in winning with ease."

-Sun Tzu, *The Art of War*

Checking the accuracy of your work is an important skill to have in chemical engineering, and one you will need to master. I can only offer a few tips on how to go about doing this, since the specifics of a given problem often dictate how to go about checking it. However, a few constraints on the correctness of any solution are always applicable:

1. Did you put your name at the top of your paper? For many professors, your name is a 100-point question.

2. Are your scientific and engineering units of measure all agreeing with each other?

3. Are you exceeding the speed of light?

4. Are you transferring heat spontaneously from cold to hot? If so, you're violating the Second Law of Thermodynamics.

5. Does your heat engine have an efficiency meeting or exceeding 100%? If so, you're violating either the First or Second Laws of Thermodynamics.

6. Are you creating or destroying energy? If so, you're violat-

ing the First Law of Thermodynamics.

7. Is the entropy of the universe decreasing? If so, you're violating the Second Law of Thermodynamics again.

8. Are you producing or destroying mass? If so, you're violating Conservation of Mass.

9. Did you calculate a temperature of 0 Kelvin or less? If so, you're violating the Third Law of Thermodynamics.

10. Did you remember to use absolute temperature when you were supposed to? Many problems require the use of absolute temperature, and the use of Celsius or Fahrenheit temperature scales will give a wrong result.

11. Does your result follow the logical, expected trend as its various parameters become extremely small or extremely large?

12. Does your heat engine exceed the Carnot efficiency? If so, it is impossible to build.

13. When dealing with probability, are your probabilities bounded over [0,1] and summing to 1?

14. Do you have exactly one equation for each unknown? If not you need to keep hunting.

15. Is your solution to the optimization problem violating the constraints?

16. Are your mole fractions bounded over [0,1] and summing to 1?

17. To reiterate, on your plant design project, are you converting expensive chemicals into cheap chemicals? If so, your process is economically infeasible.

Aside from these points, there is also the issue of answering the actual question. When many engineering students start doing their homework or working an exam problem, they do not pay attention to the actual question being asked, leading to needless computations and much wasted time. The real problem on your exams is not answering the question – it is answering the question in the most straightforward manner possible. Anyone can succeed at anything given infinite resources, but in reality infinite resources do not exist. It is one thing to spend hours working a complete mass and energy balance to finally get the answer, but it is another matter entirely to compute the desired answer in a few steps.

6.14 Dispelling "Impostor Syndrome"

"Have no fear of perfection – you'll never reach it."

-Salvador Dali

Impostor syndrome is the irrational belief that one's personal success in life – especially school – has been completely due to random chance, and that they are not nearly as smart as their accomplishments would suggest. There is a gnawing fear that eventually their true incompetence will be unmasked and everyone will know they were dealing with an impostor the whole time. I felt for a while I was an "impostor," because many things didn't seem very hard to me. But eventually reality began to set in. It was not as hard for me because I was studying a lot more than many of my classmates.

For the mathematically-minded person, some reflection on probabilities might shake them from their impostor syndrome. The claim made is that your success so far in school is due to favorable luck. This is extraordinarily unlikely. Many engineering exams are not multiple choice, making them virtually impossible to score highly on by drawing random symbols – but let's relax this assumption and assume your professors only offer multiple-choice engineering exams. Even if all of your exams you had ever taken were multiple choice, the odds of you picking the correct answer by random chance on so many exams is near-zero. For example, the probability of you getting a 100% by random chance on a twenty-five question five-choice multiple choice test is about 10^{-18}. On a given semester, you will likely have four classes with four exams each, thus making the odds exponentially lower than even that figure.

I especially felt like an impostor when I came to my first engineering job. My first day I felt overwhelmed when my boss handed me a stack of papers an inch thick explaining the problem statement for the project our group was working on. I had the "deer in the headlights" look on my face when he handed it to me, and wondered if I was cut out for the job. I was terrified my boss was going to feel "cheated" that he didn't get the quality of engineer he was paying for, that my qualifications weren't up to snuff, or that I had somehow been deceptive during the job interview. Eventually, though, I got over the problem. Talking with my boss really helped. Apparently, I wasn't the only person in our group who had this fear.

While I will probably be accused of elitism, the best thing to do with your gifts is to take ownership of them. Realize that you had no say in whether you would be born as bright as you are. The best thing to do about impostor syndrome is to shake it off and come to the probably uncomfortable realization that you really are as smart as your accomplishments would suggest, and therefore are responsible for using your great gifts and talents in a beneficiary manner.

7 Teamwork and Leadership

7.1 The Need for Teamwork on Chemical Engineering Projects

"The keystone of successful business is cooperation. Friction retards progress."

-James Cash Penney

Teamwork will be required repeatedly in your education in chemical engineering. Lab reports and projects take too much time for one person to prepare, so each person will need to be assigned a portion of the report to write. In virtually all chemical engineering undergraduate programs, senior engineering students in their final semester must present a "capstone" design project with their team, which is typically the design of a chemical plant or a chemical product, or even both. This project typically takes an entire semester to do, and will require heavy contribution from each team member to accomplish.

As a chemical engineering student, you'll need to get comfortable with teamwork. Laboratory assignments, laboratory write-ups, and semester projects are infeasible to do by yourself, and will require the help of at least one other person. Teamwork is also necessary in "the real world." While it is theoretically possible for lone garage tinkerers to come up with killer new technologies, most serious chemical engineering work requires the resources of a modern, industrial, corporate-technostate. Large engineering projects and directed research requires vast teams of highly educated people, from a variety of technical and educational backgrounds, multi-million dollar facilities, expensive computers, and pricey instrumentation. To succeed in chemical engineering, you need to be able to play well with others and work efficiently in a team setting.

I confess I have a love-hate relationship with teamwork in an academic setting. On the negative side, it makes it easy for slackers to get by in a course with meager contributions. On the positive side, requiring teamwork in a course mimics a real-world engineering job, where everything is a team effort. Working with teammates you like can be a very rewarding experience, and makes seemingly-impossible projects more manageable. Furthermore, some of your undergraduate project partners may very well end up becoming your friends for life. The difficult projects and assignments you'll have to struggle through together foster *esprit de corps* in a way difficult to describe using written words.

As far as being a good group member, you want to have the reputation as someone who brings their "A-game" every day. People who slack on their end only end up making more work for others, which rapidly breeds resentment. The free market is probably the harshest judge of your capabilities. If your fellow students don't want to work with you, that is a poor reflection on your capabilities as a chemical engineer.

7.2 Being a Good Leader for Your Teammates

"...Anyone who wants to be first must be the very last, and the servant of all."

-The New Testament, Mark 9:35

I think it is important in team settings for each team to have a specifically designated leader. Your team will probably be about three to five people, including you, making voting an ineffective method for project management. Voting is generally a horrible method of project management anyways. Lack of confidence in leadership abilities is a consistent problem I have noticed among bright engineering students. They avoid leadership positions like arsenic, fearing the mantle too heavy for their narrow shoulders. Paradoxically, these people are the ones best fit for leadership positions. If you are doing well in your classes, play competitive team sports, or have a track record of successful project execution in clubs and other organizations, you should give it a try.

Contrary to your fears, your teammates will probably not find you bossy, self-centered, or presumptuous for wanting a leadership role. More likely, they will be relieved to see someone provide firm direction. The results of poor leadership can vary wildly, but it rarely results in a satisfactory project that is completed on time. The result is mostly a great deal of stress for everyone, chaotic task delegations, repetition of already-completed work, confusion, and ultimately a poor lab report or project proposal that no one wants to read or give consideration to.

Clearly, this is a situation you want to avoid.

A leadership position comes with great responsibility. The leader is not merely someone who puts his feet up on a desk while his underlings toil. The overall formulation and execution of the plan is the leader's responsibility. The best leaders are also those who work to serve those they lead. If someone is having trouble, you help them get through it. A good leader does not ridicule, put down, or scold his subordinates. If one of your teammates does something unsatisfactory, set aside time to discuss the problem with them like two reasonable adults. Maybe they did not do very well in that subject, and did the best they could. Calling people "dumb", "stupid", or "incompetent" is not the habits of a successful, inspiring leader.

Conversely, if your teammates do a great job, let them know it. People appreciate getting pats-on-the-back when they have worked hard on something. High morale is obviously better than poor morale, and you should work hard to keep it high. People work better when they are confident their work is contributory, and that the project is going to be completed on time.

As far as learning how to be a good leader, I do not think books are capable of teaching this skill. I have read several books on leadership, and found them to be mostly baloney sprinkled with a few bits of common sense. The best way to get leadership experience is to, well, get leadership experience! Take on a project or laboratory assignment as the team lead, come up with the organized action plan for the group, and oversee its successful execution. Begin with the end in mind, and divide the major task into as many small work units as possible to hand off to your subordinates.

7.3 Advice for Teamwork on Laboratory Reports

"Plan for what it is difficult while it is easy, do what is great while it is small."

-Sun Tzu, *The Art of War*

I have noticed in the multiple laboratory classes I have taken, that the lab manual is usually not written in the most logical order for executing the lab. Before each organic chemistry lab, I would sit down with the lab manual, write out all of the steps for the lab, and look for tasks that could be done in parallel. For example, while one substance comes to a boil on the hotplate, perhaps we can collect some data on some other aspect of the experiment. Tight coordination with your lab partners can pay off heavily here, and probably will result in you finishing your laboratory early, and with better data.

This next task requires more effort, but is ultimately well worth it. You should have a complete plan on what data you will be required to collect, and what operations are going to be performed on that data when you get it. This makes it much easier to focus on collecting the data you need, and "filling in the blanks" that you've created for yourself. This can be a tricky task to come up with, and requires much abstract thinking. Ideally, before you even collect the data, you will have a set of Python, MATLAB, or Excel scripts ready-to-go that will compute all of the important quantities the lab is asking you to calculate.

7.4   Advice for the Chemical Engineering Senior Capstone Project

"Of all the things I've done, the most vital is coordinating the talents of those who work for us and pointing them towards a certain goal."

-Walt Disney

A rite of passage in chemical engineering education is the final "capstone" project required in the senior year of school, where students must either design a chemical product, or a chemical process facility. Some students opt to do both; they design a new product, and also present how it would be feasibly mass-produced. This project is the culmination of all learning in school up to this point, including mass and energy balances, thermodynamics, control systems, engineering optimization, and economic analysis. This is a daunting challenge that many undergraduates dread and can immobilize them with fear.

At USF, to add extra pressure to the ordeal, projects were presented in the form of posters before the Industrial Advisory Board and the faculty. The board was composed mainly of local senior engineers employed in the chemicals industry. Projects were marketed as investments, and pitched to potential investors – and potential investors are probably the toughest crowd someone can ever face. We were grilled quite a bit.

One of the interesting things about the project is the immense freedom your team has in defining your problem, and how you go about solving it. I saw a wide array of projects back in 2008 when I was working on my own senior design project, and again in 2010 when I was assigned to be a judge during the poster competition. Offhand, some of the projects I can remember were: the conversion of sugar-cane waste biomass to gasoline; the production of biopharmaceuticals using fermentation; and the catalytic cracking of petroleum. This freedom is both a blessing and a curse, as students are used to being told what the problem is, given all the data, and being ask to solve it. For this assignment, students are tasked with coming up with their own problem, hunting down their own data, and then solving their problem themselves.

One can get a general idea as to the scale of the problem by consulting the American Institute of Chemical Engineers Senior Project Competition website [60]. In high school you are used to working problems that perhaps occupy a single line on a page, maybe a paragraph. These problem statements run about twenty pages[16] . This is done intentionally to drive home the point that you have no hope of solving such a problem on your own, and will need to marshal the resources of a team to accomplish the task within the semester.

I am limited in what advice I can give for the senior capstone project, since the specific course of action will depend heavily on what your project actually is. Your plant design textbook will discuss the general strategy of process synthesis, so it is not necessary to regurgitate that here. The best strategy for dividing up the labor is to develop a general plan of action that divides the project into many smaller tasks, and assign responsibilities based on each team member's strengths. As far as teamwork goes, I reiterate the need for a designated leader. The leader should probably be the most technically-competent person of the group, who can bolster the other teammates should they get stuck on something. The leader oversees not only the technical aspects of the project, but also the write-up, poster layout, and the PowerPoint presentation if applicable.

---

[16] And it only gets worse in the real world! At my first engineering job, on the very first day of work, my boss handed me a stack of white papers describing the problem statement for our current project that was about an inch thick. It took me about two months to get anywhere just grasping the actual problem.

BALANCING ACT

The senior capstone project will probably be the most difficult thing you do in undergraduate chemical engineering, but you should not dread it. The project is quite do-able, provided you work hard and consistently as a team on it. The most difficult part of the project is breaking the enormous project down into a series of concrete, manageable tasks, and semi-accurately assigning a time frame for each task. Obviously, the sum of all task times needs to fall within the project deadline.

I emphasize that the tasks need to be concrete. Avoid tasks such as "Learn how a crystallizer works," – this task is too open-ended as it is written; it has no clearly defined start and end point. One could study crystallizers for the remainder of their natural life and not learn everything there is to know about them. This task needs to be broken down further. Perhaps instead of "Learn how a crystallizer works," you might instead use several tasks (in no particular order):

- Estimate the required volume of our crystallizer. 1 day.

- Write the full mass, energy, and population balance equations for the crystallizer. 3 days.

- Design a control system for the crystallizer. 5 days.

- Write a dynamic model of the crystallizer and implement it in Simulink. 4 days.

- Find out how 'purity' is quantified regarding crystallizer products. ½ a day.

- Decide on whether to use batch or continuous crystallization for our project. 3 days.

Each of these tasks has a definitive answer or result, which can be used to push the project forward, and are far more useful than simply "Learn how a crystallizer works." There are also time limits on the tasks, clearly stating how much time has been budgeted to that task.

8 Preserving Your Health

8.1 To Maintain Good Mental Health, Maintain Good Physical Health

"In health there is freedom. Health is the first of all liberties."

-Henri Frederic Amiel

Engineering school is very taxing upon the mind and body. There is constant need to study and review prior material, and new material is always being thrown at you. Burnout and depression are serious problems among students in engineering and the hard sciences. I myself struggled greatly with depression during my doctoral studies. However, there are some significant actions you can take to preserve your health throughout school.

For starters, get regular exercise. I worked out pretty consistently throughout my undergraduate studies, and it was a real life-saver. Hitting the weights for thirty to forty-five minutes three times a week, and doing thirty to forty-five minutes of cardio every weekday is a great way to stay in shape, relieve stress, and control your weight. It also – at least for me – has a curative effect on the mood and mind. Getting regular exercise can also help you stay on a regular sleep schedule.

Getting adequate sleep is especially important when undertaking such a difficult major as chemical engineering. You need to get to sleep at a decent time, and get a full eight hours. I personally had awful problems with sleep during my doctoral studies, which even heavy exercise couldn't resolve, and required professional help. If you have this problem, I urge you to get professional help.

Eating a healthy diet is a great way to improve your mood and your health. Avoid the temptation to eat the garbage food available at the campus cafeteria; focus on the healthy options. Lean meats, vegetables, yogurt, and fruit are good choices. Avoid eating at least three hours before bed time. Avoid gaining excess weight. I gained a ton of weight during my doctoral studies, which I am now in the process of losing. I am confident I will be able to lose the weight, but it didn't have to be that way. Avoid stress eating. If you catch yourself stress eating, stop.

8.2 Preventing Academic Burnout

"Learned helplessness is the giving-up reaction, the quitting response that follows from the belief that whatever you do doesn't matter."

-Arnold Schwarzenegger

Academic burnout is a sudden loss of interest in schooling due to fatigue from intensive study and high-stakes examinations. Much like muscle fatigue when lifting weights, burnout comes on suddenly even when you were at first going strong. Burnout is a major problem in engineering school. The constant drudgery of doing math for several hours a day, reading and studying difficult material, and the dread of exams, takes its toll on you after a while. It is that way on purpose as a way to get rid of people who aren't serious. There have been many times I wanted to quit, which actually is a good sign. If you are putting forth the effort needed to succeed at a high level in engineering school, you are going to want to quit at some point. When you want to quit, you're about halfway there. Embrace the suck.

There are countermeasures, though, which can minimize the chance of burning out. I again recommend regular exercise. More important is having a set of fun routines that you get to enjoy every week, which allow you to let your hair down and not think about school for a few hours. I would go to the gym to blow off steam, and go play Magic with friends on Tuesdays and Thursdays. On the weekends, with no exams in sight, I would study lightly and play video games. Every so often, friends and I would go out to eat together. If there was a movie worth seeing, I would go see it. Sometimes I would go to the library to find a book to read, purely out of curiosity, and not because I was going to be given an exam on the subject. To summarize, it is important to have multiple weekly diversions that give your brain a rest from the daily grind.

Some people succumb to the temptation to "take a break" from school and take a semester off. I strongly recommend against this. There is too much risk that you will not return to school, or will forget critical material. There is no way around this: the easiest way to get through chemical engineering is to do it non-stop for four years.

Another quick path to burnout is to get off of a regular sleep schedule. You must discipline yourself to get to bed at a decent time and wake up at a reasonable hour. Daily studying plays a part in this. Studying daily will tire your mind out, making it easier to fall asleep. Furthermore, daily study is far more effective than all-night cramming-with-Red Bull sessions. Strongly resist the temptation to stay up all night studying. It will destroy your sleep schedule and render you a zombie during the exam. Self-discipline is a skill you must master in engineering school. There is no way around it.

8.3 Keep All Options Open Regarding Your Mental Health

"Coming home from very lonely places, all of us go a little mad: whether from great personal success, or just an all-night drive, we are the sole survivors of a world no one else has ever seen."

-John Le Carre

If you feel like you "just can't take it anymore," go see the campus psychiatric services. Depending on the results of the little quiz they give you, they will probably prescribe you some kind of anti-anxiety or anti-depressant medication. These medications did wonders for my mental health during my doctoral studies. As a bonus, they also fixed the tremendous sleep problems that had been troubling me for years.

If you move to a very cold winter climate for school (e.g. West Lafayette), the sky is overcast for much of the winter, and the lack of visible sunlight can lead to mental health problems. "Seasonal affective disorder (SAD)" is a type of depression common among people who live in areas with long, bleak winters. The problem can be kept under control through medication, and also by use of a "happy lamp," a special type of lamp which exudes bright, sunshine-like light. Staring at this lamp for a few minutes every day can help get the problems of SAD under control.

8.4 Keep Friends Within Reach

"Friendship is born at that moment when one person says to another, 'What! You too? I thought I was the only one.'"

-C.S. Lewis

Socialization is key to good mental health. Get involved in some sort of group activity outside of school. This was a major tactical error I made for about half of my time at Purdue. I constantly felt alone, which compounded my depression. I would go to the gym occasionally, but never really met any friends there. Intramural sports are a great way to get some exercise and human contact outside of school. A church group on campus would fit someone who frequently undertakes daunting trials of religious introspection. I started going to a local game store[17] in mid-2012 to find people to play Magic the Gathering with. Many of the store's denizens were other graduate students at Purdue, which expanded my circle of friends. I eventually made it a weekly habit to go to Friday Night Magic at the shop to get more human contact outside of school. I eventually started attending Tuesday and Thursday night casual Magic as well, of which I have many fond memories. There are fewer more enjoyable simple pleasures than playing cards with some buddies, cracking jokes, bantering back and forth, commiserating about graduate school, and otherwise shooting the bull with each other for a few hours each week.

If your fellow students are going to put on some kind of event, then you should make plans to attend it. This is especially true in graduate school, where work so frequently subsumes your available free time. While it was always tempting to stay back in my apartment, I never regretted going out with the group for fun activities, such as laser tag, or having Thanksgiving dinner together in the fall of 2014. Those are memories I will always cherish.

8.5 Bad Relationships with the Opposite Sex

"It is far better to be alone, than to be in bad company."

-George Washington

An especially pernicious influence on mental health deserves special attention. Be cautious with your romantic relationships, and what boyfriends or girlfriends you choose to deal with. When I went to the

---

[17] The Sages' Shoppe is a family-owned game store in West Lafayette, Indiana, run by Chad and Jennifer Fauber. If you're down for some Magic, its one of the best shops I've ever attended in terms of atmosphere and available play area.

psychiatric services clinic at Purdue, I was given a quiz on why I was seeking help for my depression. About 80% of the questions on the quiz were related to problems with a romantic partner, or some kind of chaos in the respondent's love life. I question the worth of having a girlfriend in college, due to high risk and comparatively little reward. While a nice girlfriend would have been beneficial, I had seen too many of my male friends put through hell by downright evil, crazy women. I've also seen nice girls get pregnant and dumped. Don't be a sucker and let that happen to you!

Do not get involved in any domestic disputes with your partner. Get off-world, off-planet, off-dimension; do whatever you have to do to get away if they start getting loud and argumentative with you; you can't win that game. If your romantic partner is getting involved in illegal drugs or heavy alcohol use, it is time to pull the plug. They are on a self-destructive path, and you run the risk of getting taken down with them. You do not want to have to explain to potential employers during job interviews why you have a drug arrest on your record, and they will not be sympathetic to your excuse that "It was all their fault!" If your romantic partner lies to you, then it is also time to move on to greener pastures. In short, while a good partner can be a great asset to you, a bad partner can drive you absolutely crazy.

I'll pass on some useful advice my mother gave to me when I was an undergraduate: "Now is the time to be selfish, Brad." And she was right. You should be selfish with your time when you are pursuing something as difficult as engineering school. Why bring all of this extra work and headache on yourself by bringing some other person into your life to create a relationship, which – judging from my observations – is probably not going to last more than eighteen months? Letting other people, especially romantic partners, into your personal sphere is a major risk that can damage your career prospects. What if that "great new girlfriend" or boyfriend of yours starts a fight the night before a major exam, puts you on tilt, and causes you to flunk the exam? When you are out of engineering school and cranking in the big bucks, then you might consider pursuing a stable relationship. To summarize: be selfish! Now is the best time to act that way. Play your cards close to your chest!

8.6 Don't Compare Yourself to Others

"Nothing in the world is worth having or worth doing unless it means effort, pain, difficulty... I have never in my life envied a human being who led an easy life. I have envied a great many people who led difficult lives and led them well."

-Teddy Roosevelt

Resist the urge to compare yourself to others. This was an extremely bad habit I had back in high school and my early years of college. I would constantly put myself down, saying things to myself such as, "I'm not as smart as that guy, I need to work harder," or "I need to spend more time in the gym. Then I can look like that guy." Of course, I'm all for self-improvement, but doing so out of covetousness is a recipe for insanity.

Not only is it a bad habit, it is also counterproductive; it limits your performance to the people surrounding you. There will always be someone smarter, stronger, faster, and just plain "better" than yourself. Just accept it, and do the best work that you can. Even if you're not the absolute best-of-the-best, you still have a lot to offer mankind and society with a chemical engineering education, and can do well for yourself.

Focus on doing the best job you can, with the resources you have available. Keep your nose to the grindstone. There just aren't enough hours in the day to become an expert at every skill in existence. Figure out what you are good at, and refine that skill until it is razor sharp. Excellence is always rewarded in the end.

9 What Chemical Engineering Graduate School is All About

9.1 The Goal of Graduate School

"I will either find a way, or make one."

-Hannibal of Carthage

In your final year of undergraduate education, if you have high enough grades – among other things[18] – you can apply to a graduate program and attempt to earn a master's or PhD. In this section, I will focus mainly on PhD programs. But what actually goes on in chemical engineering graduate school? What do the students and professors do all day?

The overarching goal of a doctoral program, as far as the student is concerned, is to graduate with their PhD. Unlike your undergraduate degree however, which depends merely on completing a battery of difficult engineering courses, graduate school has the added bonus of requiring research publications. Aside from a more difficult course load and several qualifying exams, the great task in graduate school is to publish as many peer-reviewed research articles in high-impact journals as possible within four or five years. A good number of first-author publications to shoot for is three. I was only able to get out two, but some students are exceptionally productive and can graduate with five or more publications [61], [62].

To accompany you in your quest to obtain a PhD, you will choose a professor in the department to serve as your academic adviser. The professor will have a general project outlined for you. One-tenth of the bone will be exposed from the earth, and your job will be to dig up the

---

[18] You need a high GRE score, recommendations from professors, and other evidence of scholarly achievement. Having published papers already on your record from undergraduate research work is a very big plus.

remaining nine-tenths. The purpose of an adviser is very much like a master tradesman is to an apprentice. He's there to offer advice and guidance on how to perform the trade. The only difference is that we're doing scientific research instead of carpentry or plumbing.

9.2 National Science Foundation Fellowships

"While money can't buy happiness, it certainly lets you choose your own form of misery."

-Groucho Marx

During my second semester at Purdue, our professors strongly encouraged us to apply for National Science Foundation (NSF) Fellowships. NSF Fellowships are prestigious, highly-sought-after four-year grants from the federal government to pay your salary during your time in graduate school – among other things. They restricted to U.S. citizens and permanent residents [63]. Getting an NSF Fellowship is basically manna from heaven in the world of graduate school. If you score an NSF Fellowship, you can work for any professor in the department, even ones who don't have any grant money coming in. After all, they're not paying you – the Feds are. Furthermore, NSF Fellowships by themselves look great on a resume. I found out the hard way that by doing my master's degree at USF I had disqualified myself from getting an NSF Fellowship. This was a tactical error on my part, and had I known about the importance of these fellowships, I would not have bothered with doing my master's degree at USF.

NSF Fellowships, however, are not disbursed on the basis of merit any longer – or at least, merit is not the primary consideration. From my observations, the strongest determinant of getting an NSF Fellowship is being a woman, being Hispanic, or being both simultaneously. I know of only one white male graduate student at Purdue who won an NSF Fellowship, but I can think of four females off the top of my head. The female graduate students pretty much said the same thing. While NSF does want to hear about your planned research, they are far more interested in your "struggles as a woman in a male-dominated atmosphere such as engineering." Likewise with my office mate from Puerto Rico, who was advised to play up being Hispanic as much as possible. These tactics worked, and they won NSF Fellowships. As one of my white male colleagues in the department said after his proposal was rejected by NSF, "My dream is to be reincarnated as a wheelchair-bound black lesbian."

9.3   Published Papers and You

"Anyone who stops learning is old, whether at twenty or eighty. Anyone who keeps learning stays young."

-Henry Ford

We'll take a brief break from the subject of graduate school to discuss these strange animals called "research articles." Peer-reviewed articles, also known as "journal articles," "published papers," or simply, "papers," are the method by which scholars in the sciences and engineering communicate their findings to their peers. "Peer-review" means two other anonymous, qualified people have read the manuscript and agreed independently to accept the article into the journal. The definition of a "high impact" journal is one with a high "impact factor." The "impact factor" is the average number of citations received by the papers in the journal within the last five years [64].

Journal articles are an arduous task to write, proofread, and collaborate upon. The papers on your record that carry the most weight are those with yourself as the first author. In order to be the first author on the publication, you must do the vast bulk of the experimental work, data analysis, and writing. The more articles you have, the happier your professor and your doctoral committee will be. Papers add weight to your PhD, since each paper is an independent, third-party attestation from outside of your own department and your own university that you are a competent researcher. Publications also add weight to a grant proposal. If you win the grant, you can get lots of money from the government to do the kind of research you want to see done. As a bonus, if you have multiple published papers, you have already written the bulk of your dissertation. Each paper serves as a chapter of your thesis. All that remains then near the end of your studies is to write a literature review and a conclusion.

Publishing papers is the lifeblood of a professor. They are used in hiring, tenure, and grant approval decisions. With so much riding on producing research, it is understandable why they are particularly keen on seeing you produce as many papers as possible. A professor's Hirsch index, or "h-index," in the academic world is the equivalent of lean muscle mass in the bodybuilding world. The h-index is a number indicating a researcher has at least h publications that each have at least h citations. Having a single "runaway hit" paper does little to change one's h-index. It is debatable how useful of a metric the h-index is, but nonetheless it is generally the metric by which a researcher's productivity is perceived.

9.4   The Importance of Citing Your Sources

"I've been imitated so well I've heard people copy my mistakes."

-Jimi Hendrix

If your education is anything like mine in the public school system, doing research papers was typically a boring chore where your English teacher flagellated you over not citing your sources properly. Most high school students do not give a rat's rear end about citations or scholarly attribution. This is not the way things work in the academic world. Properly citing your sources is mandatory, since the price of plagiarism is the cost of your professional reputation. Citations are, theoretically, evidence that your fellow researchers are producing useful research. If you take ideas from a paper and do not cite it properly, you are not only stealing, you are also denying due credit, and the rewards thereof, to a peer. Citations are a big deal when publishing papers; they are the main metric by how research value is quantified. In fact, there is a whole branch of mathematical investigation devoted to statistically measuring the impact of journal papers via citation analysis [65].

9.5   How Graduate Students and Professors Spend Their Time

"A professor is someone who talks in someone else's sleep."

-W.H. Auden

Now that we understand what the goal of graduate school is, it is easy to see what students do all day. They are trying to produce original research that they can write up into a journal paper. Many activities are done in furtherance of this goal, such as running and designing experiments, fixing busted lab equipment, ordering chemicals, characterizing materials, growing cells and bacteria, writing computer code, analyzing data, collaborating with other graduate students, reading the academic literature, attending required classes, studying for class, writing up notes on results and literature findings, and having progress meetings with their major professor. Every few semesters the student will have teaching responsibilities, such as grading papers and giving lectures to undergraduate students. Most graduate students are out of school a few weeks out of the year to attend academic conferences. Graduate students that have met all of the departmental requirements and published several papers are ready to graduate, and spend their time writing up their dissertation. A dissertation is basically a compendium of the research you have produced during your time at the university. The exact structure of the document varies, but the basic layout is a literature review, followed by individual research contributions – which are more or less the content of your published papers) – and ended with a conclusion and directions for future research.

What do professors do all day? Mainly teaching. But the remainder of their day is filled with research-focused activities, such as discussing research with other professors, thinking up grant proposal ideas, writing papers and books, meeting with students, making plans for the summer, writing grant proposals, attending scholarly committees, and consulting with industrial partners. It is common for professors to take a sabbatical to either attend a different university and acquire new skills, or to use their sabbatical to write a book. Some professors have spun off their research into private technology start-up companies, and spend much of their time managing their business affairs and pitching the company to potential investors [66], [67].

10 Student Loans and You

10.1 The High Cost of College Attendance

"The only reason a great many American families don't own an elephant is that they have never been offered an elephant for a dollar down and easy weekly payments."

-MAD Magazine

I mentioned student loans briefly in section 1, and I think greater discussion of these abominations is necessary for the hapless high school student. From a high level perspective, America is a country addicted to debt: student loan debt is about $1.2 trillion, which exceeds total credit card debt and total auto loan debt [68]. As of the year 2016, 66% of student borrowers graduating with only a bachelor's degree are expected to leave school with about $35,000 in debt [69]. Bottom line, your degree in engineering is probably going to cost you at least $35,000, and will cost much more if you take longer to graduate. Assuming you start off at $80,000 a year, lose 25% to taxes, put $18,000 into your company retirement account – which you should – and live off $25,000 a year, that leaves about $17,000 of disposable income. Assuming a student loan debt amount of $35,000 represents about a two year payoff time, which is quite reasonable. Student loan affordability is often defined as "paid off within ten years." To get a realistic idea of how much you can safely borrow, look at your expected yearly income from the four-year degree you have chosen – that is your debt ceiling. For example, if you can expect to make $80,000 per year with a computer science degree, then you have a maximum debt ceiling of $80,000.

10.2 Out of Control Borrowing for Worthless Degrees

"An empty head leads to an empty pocket."

-B.C. Forbes

Some people have much higher student loan balances, sometimes reaching comical heights. I've read multiple horror stories of people who have borrowed up to $250,000 for a degree, only to find they can only get jobs for perhaps $35,000-$40,000 per year. One young woman was a single mother who graduated with a useless degree in social work and monstrously high student loan debt. Her monthly minimum payment was over $900, comparable to my rent. For perspective, my monthly minimum is about $130. One none-too-bright young man borrowed over $250,000 for law school, but could only find work as a prosecutor for the city of New York, which paid about $35,000 per year. He is now leading a reform movement for the nationalization of student loan debt ("nationalization" means the taxpayer pays for it). One gentleman racked up $35,000 in student loans to obtain a prized master's degree in ... puppetry [70].

10.3 Paying the Money Back

"The only man who sticks closer to you in adversity than a friend is a creditor."

-Unknown

Once you graduate – or drop out – the bank and/or the federal government will be at your door with their palm out, demanding their money back. Except in extraordinary circumstances (e.g. being rendered a quadriplegic), it is impossible to discharge student loan debt in bankruptcy court. This puts student loan debts in the same category as child support obligations, criminal fines, and victim restitution payments [71]. Like a case of herpes, they are stuck on you. Don't even bother trying to re-negotiate a student loan after the fact. The loan company is holding all the cards, and has the might of the state behind them. They do not have to make deals with someone who has nothing to bargain with. Decide to quit paying? They'll garnish your wages, steal your income tax return, nab your social security payments, and drag your butt to court to get their money. The Mafia is more likely to renegotiate a loan with you than a student loan creditor.

"Forbearance" is another "gotcha" the banks like to spring on people. If you cannot pay your student loans, they will gladly offer to put your student loan into forbearance, meaning you don't have to make any payments for a certain number of years. This is an extremely bad move. While you do not need to make payments, interest will continue to accrue on the debt load, meaning you will be paying even more after the forbearance expires. Don't fall for that trick!

When you go to get a student loan, be sure to read and understand all the documents you are given. Do not rely on the loan issuer to explain what the documents are saying; he is not paid to act as your advocate. This responsibility is up to you. Also, do not be cajoled or arm-twisted by your parents into taking on huge debt-levels. This is a recurring theme in many of the student loan horror stories I have read. There is absolutely no rush to enroll into college, especially when you are unsure of what major you want to pursue. You must keep your debt level under control, and understand just how high the stakes are if you need to borrow for your college education.

10.4   The Dysfunctional Nature of College Funding

"Everybody's youth is a dream, a form of chemical madness."

-F. Scott Fitzgerald

It is worth reflecting on how dysfunctional our higher education funding system is in America. Many college freshmen enter the campus at the age of seventeen, and are legally barred from a whole host of activities. They cannot drink or buy alcohol, vote in elections, operate an automobile, own firearms, be employed outside of a family business, have sex (depending on the state), join the military, get married (depending on the state), run for public office, gamble, or buy or use tobacco products. As minors they usually cannot be held to the same standard of responsibility in a criminal case due to their young age. Being unable to legally work, virtually all credit card companies will reject any application they submit due to having zero income. American society has multiple sanctions in place to, theoretically, protect people below the age of eighteen, under the assumption that their minds are not fully developed and cannot be expected to act in their own best interests. But this same seventeen year old, who is otherwise a child in the eyes of the law, can be dragged with their parents to a student loan vendor, quickly sign a few papers they did not read, and suddenly indebt themselves for tens of thousands of dollars, despite not even having a job or any other source of income! What kind of sense does that make!?

10.5 Options for Avoiding Debt Slavery

"The rich rule over the poor, and the borrower is slave to the lender."

-The Old Testament, Proverbs 22:7

In summary, student loans are the work of the devil, and are probably the biggest expense you will ever take out in life other than a house. High student loan debt is a source of much misery in America today. There are people in this country so deep in student loan debt, that based upon their maximum likely salary in their chosen profession, will mathematically never be able to pay it off. As a historical reflection, it is ironic that America fought a horrific civil war in order to free blacks from slavery, at a cost of hundreds of thousands of Billy Yanks and Johnny Rebs, only for legions of Americans to wind up in financial suzerainty to the banks. Historically, African-Americans even celebrate June 19, 1865, as "Juneteenth," the date that slavery was formally ended in America. Yet today, millions of Americans are de facto debt slaves. Black, white, or brown, the banks manacle them all – and unlike a plantation master, the bank does not have to provide you with room and board. While it is nice to dream, in our current political system, I am not looking forward to any "student debt Juneteenth" to be headed our way any time soon – and you shouldn't expect such a miracle either.

The purpose of this section is not to strike fear into you that student loans will ruin your life, as there are times where it makes sense to take on debt in order to secure a higher return. I just want you go into this with both eyes open, and not be sent off to die like some pitiful British soldier at the Somme in 1916. If you are uncomfortable taking on a high level of debt, but still want to go to college, you have three – and not mutually exclusive – options: join the military and get Uncle Sam to pay for it, work and save up money to fund your own education, and/or acquire scholarship money.

There are significant risks and much hardship associated with military life, which you will need to think carefully about before signing up. Working and saving up money will make your education take much longer, but will keep the debt load down. Scholarships are the weapon of choice for the intelligent, energetic young person interested in upward mobility. If your state offers a scholarship for good school performance, then you should definitely obtain it. For example, the state of Florida has the Bright Futures Scholarship, funded by the Florida Lottery. Apply aggressively for scholarship money. Many scholarships are exclusively for racial minorities. If you happen to be a member of such a minority group, you should apply to any minority-specific scholarship you are eligible for. Check your family history, and be absolutely sure you are not Hispanic. Hispanics are eligible for enormous amounts of scholarship aid that other races have zero access to.

11 Avoiding a Criminal Record

This chapter should not be construed as specific legal advice. Even slight differences between scenarios can have different legal ramifications. For legal advice, you should talk to an attorney.

11.1 The Problem of Out-of-Control Police Officers

"A recent police study found that you're much more likely to get shot by a fat cop if you run."

-Dennis Miller

This relevance of this chapter might puzzle some readers. "What do the police have to do with chemical engineering?" you might ask yourself. Unfortunately, a lot I'm afraid. The career consequences of bad police interactions cannot be overstated, and you don't want to get on their bad side. If you get a felony arrest, felony conviction, or a drug conviction, you might as well throw in the towel on engineering school – no one will hire you. I have applied to jobs that didn't even bother asking about convictions – instead they asked "Have you ever been arrested on a felony charge?" If you check that box, your application will get trashed before the hiring manager even sees it. There are no "do-overs" when it comes to dealing with the police, and they play for keeps.

To further expound upon the career consequences of a criminal record, most government contractors are strictly against hiring people with records. This goes double for positions that require a security clearance, such as defense work, or working in a government lab. Many states will not allow you pursue professional engineering licensure with a felony record. If you get a felony DUI, you can cross off any position that would put you in control of dangerous, expensive equipment. Likewise with a theft conviction and any position that would have you handle large sums of money, such as a management position. You might as well move to Mars if you have a sex offender conviction.

A bad cop can ruin your life. Not all policemen are bad people, but this is irrelevant. Sometimes, police departments suffer serious lapses in judgment of who they choose to hire. Some cops are violent thugs. Some are psychologically unsound. Some can look into a jury's eyes with the demeanor of a saint and tell them a lie. Some are cynical careerists that have no qualms about locking up an innocent person. You have no idea what kind of cop you are dealing with out-of-the-box, and can't see the halos above anyone's head.

The conjecture that bad cops are a serious problem in American police forces is supported by quantitative evidence. In 2015, the ten cities with the largest police departments in America paid out nearly a quarter billion dollars in judgments and settlements resulting from police misconduct [72]. Since 2010, those same cities have paid out over a billion dollars in judgments. Many agencies have special insurance policies that kick in specifically for payments resulting from police misconduct – and the taxpayer foots the bill for it all. The city of Chicago has resorted to borrowing hundreds of millions of dollars to pay for the misdeeds of its out-of-control officers [73]. Payouts have increased dramatically in recent years. The proliferation of cell phones equipped with live video-streaming capabilities is likely responsible for some of this increase. Another possible reason is that the unconscionably light punishments meted out to bad police officers fail to deter their misconduct, emboldening them to commit more of it [74]. It remains to be seen if these payments will ever become political issues for taxpayers, and eventually lead to changes in how police departments are run and how officers are trained. Nonetheless, the best policy for you now is to play a good defensive game when dealing with the police.

This chapter is most relevant (in terms of the law) to readers in the United States, but foreign readers should also heed the advice in this chapter. Hiring practices are likely the same in your country as they are in America, and that means companies that do engineering work are highly averse to hiring people with criminal records. Many foreign readers probably have aspirations of moving to America to do engineering work. You will need to remain squeaky clean if you want to have a shot at coming to America to work or study.

11.2 Your Constitutional Rights

"We the People of the United States, in Order to form a more perfect Union, establish Justice, insure domestic Tranquility, provide for the common defence, promote the general Welfare, and secure the Blessings of Liberty to ourselves and our Posterity, do ordain and establish this Constitution for the United States of America."

-The Preamble to the U.S. Constitution

There are ways to avoid negative police interactions. Unlike in many other countries, the legal deck actually starts off stacked heavily in your favor. The U.S. Constitution presents an enormous barrier to arresting and prosecuting you. The Founding Fathers were serious about keeping people out of jail, unless the evidence against the accused was overwhelming and gathered lawfully. The Constitutional freedoms most relevant when dealing with the police are the Fourth, Fifth, and Sixth Amendments, which grant the rights [75]:

- Protection against being compelled to be a witness against yourself. This means you do not have to talk to the police, and cannot be forced to testify at a trial.

- Protection against "unreasonable" searches and seizures of your person or property.

- Protection against double jeopardy. This means if the state wants to prosecute you for a crime, they only get one chance to do it. This is to prevent the prosecutor from being able to guarantee a conviction by trying the case enough times to eventually get a jury sympathetic to his arguments.

- The right to a speedy, public trial, the right to confront the witnesses against you, and the right to consult legal counsel for your defense. This required transparency prevents the state from simply conjuring "witnesses" out of thin air, and concocting evidence to use against you. Furthermore, you are legally allowed to have an attorney do all of the talking for you at trial or with the police.

These rights make it extremely difficult to convict anybody in America. The problem with these rights, is that it is up to you to exercise them. This is why the criminal justice system is a bloated leviathan: people are ignorant of their Constitutional rights, voluntarily waive their rights, or give in to police intimidation and mind games to get them to waive their rights.

11.3 The Legal "Magic Words"

"...the clever combatant imposes his will on the enemy, but does not allow the enemy's will to be imposed on him."

-Sun Tzu, *The Art of War*

While television shows such as *Law and Order* and *CSI* have romanticized forensic evidence, the most usual method the police use to secure a conviction is to get the suspect to confess. Obviously, confessions look very bad in front of a jury. Any competent lawyer will advise his clients to never speak to the police under any circumstances. Answering a police officer's questions is always counter to your self-interests. Do not talk to the police, except to say the "magic words":

"I do not consent to any searches or seizures. I want to speak to an attorney. I have nothing further to say. Am I free to go now?"

Saying these magic words is the Star Trek equivalent of "Shields up!" It automatically makes the officer's job very difficult. The officer will likely respond to this statement by attempting to downplay or ignore it, or try to convince you that you aren't in any "real trouble." He may also laugh and ridicule you, to get you to believe the words mean nothing. If you remain steadfast, the officer will likely become irritated and aggressive with you, in order to intimidate you into compliance. He also may become more deferential, as he knows he is dealing with someone who isn't ignorant of their rights. Another tactic is, once you assert your rights, is for the police to accuse you of an enormous crime to excite you and put pressure on you to "clear your name." Let them accuse you all day long – being accused of a crime is not the same as being prosecuted for one.

Do not answer confrontational questions such as "Do you want to go to jail?" Do not give in and start talking. Simply repeat the magic words. Also, do not remain silent without saying the magic words. The U.S. Supreme Court, in its vast unwisdom, has decided that remaining silent without specifically invoking the Fifth Amendment protections can be introduced into court as evidence of guilt [76]. Never sign any documents the police offer to you, or write anything down they ask you to write – other than to sign a traffic ticket. You are only braiding the rope they will hang you with.

Refusing to speak to the police is more difficult than it sounds. It is a myth that police officers are dumb, at least when it comes to human psychology, and the detectives that do interrogations are very sharp. Higher-ranking officers are often required to have a college degree. Professional interrogators are experts at mind games, and are specially trained to get people to waive their rights and confess. There are all sorts of tricks they can use to gain your cooperation. Interrogation rooms – nowadays called "interview rooms" – are intentionally uncomfortable and small, and the chairs are often uncomfortable as well. This is to make you want to do something – anything – to get out of that place. The detective, contrary to intuition, will not browbeat you, but will try to approach you as a friend looking out for your best interests. He may also try to approach you as a "teammate," who just wants to "get to the bottom of things." The detective can also play the "waiting game," by spending as much time as he wants in the interrogation room. He is getting paid generous overtime to be in that room, and can sit there as long as it takes to get you to start talking. Sometimes the interrogator won't say anything, as they know people hate silence and will start talking just to make conversation. Nonetheless, all of the interrogator's training and tricks are useless if you just keep repeating the magic words.

The magic words also cover searches. Legally, if the police want to search and seize property, they must get a judge to issue a warrant by convincing him that there is likely to be contraband or incriminating evidence in a certain well-defined geographic area. However, police often do not need warrants for a variety of reasons. Probably the biggest exception is the "plain view rule." If a crime is committed in "plain view" of a police officer, he does not need a warrant to search and seize property related to the crime, or to pursue a suspect on foot. Regardless of these exceptions, you should never consent to a search. Even if you have nothing to hide, the officer can damage your property or smash items to look inside for contraband. Good luck getting compensated for anything he breaks.

The right to having a public trial works in your favor. Most prosecutors are not interested in going to trial, due to their high caseload and the enormous expense, labor, and time it takes to prepare for court. He also needs to do a good job, because your lawyer can exploit any slip-up on the part of the prosecutor during the appeals process. Prosecutors enjoy open-and-shut cases, where the evidence against the accused is overwhelming and damning, allowing them to negotiate a tough plea deal. However, if you have exercised your rights fully, there is likely not much direct evidence against you, making the prosecutor more likely to drop the case.

11.4 Advice for General Situations

"The lips of fools bring them strife, and their mouths invite a beating. The mouths of fools are their undoing, and their lips are a snare to their very lives."

-The Old Testament, Proverbs 18:6-7

Mutual respect goes a long way to ending a police encounter quickly. If you treat a policeman with respect, he'll probably treat you with respect, and be disinclined to give you a rough time. If you lose your patience and become angry, you'll regret it. Don't talk back or argue with a policeman, no matter how wrong he is. Police are generally clean-cut, middle-class people, so presenting yourself in the same manner is a wise move.

Do not get into a car with anyone you suspect has used drugs, or might have drugs on them. Police do profile people, especially a car full of four young college-age kids. A police officer seeing such a vehicle riding around automatically thinks "I bet at least one of them has weed on them." If one of your friends does have drugs on them, you'd better remove that wristwatch because those cuffs are coming on. Get sent to jail? You'll have to withdrawal from all your classes, and will lose any grant or scholarship support you had with a drug conviction.

I reiterate my previous suggestion: pull the plug on social media. Don't blab your personal business all over the internet. It is not difficult for the police to get access to your text messages or social media posts, and such evidence is freely admissible in court. Even the most innocuous post can be presented in a damning way by a skilled prosecutor. Don't talk about who you're sleeping with, how much money you make, where you've been, where you're going, or anything related to these things. Social media is where promising careers go to die.

Don't ever open the door for a police officer to your home or dorm room. The police will often use intimidation tactics to get you to comply, such as shouting "Police! Open up!" Don't fall for it, and don't open the door. It is easy for a police officer to barge in, and then claim afterwards that you invited him into your home, or that he "thought he smelled marijuana." The situation becomes more complicated if the police claim to have a warrant, in which case you should probably open the door for them – otherwise, they will break it down.

Understand how your cell phone works. Many cell phones come with encryption software, which you should use. Encryption scrambles the data on the phone, and can then only be decrypted with the correct password. With a decent password, the data on the phone will be strongly protected. Never give the password to anyone. Bear in mind however, that while the data on your phone may be protected, data you send to other computer systems probably will not be encrypted – especially social media servers and your friends' cell phones. If you encrypt your phone, but your friend doesn't, the police will be able to recover all of your shared text messages. Never send a text message you don't want to be read to a jury. Never consent to a police search of your phone. This same advice goes for your laptop or tablet. Always encrypt your personal data.

In the event of a terror attack or mass shooting, the police often flatly disregard the Constitution and due process, and will deal with any challenge to their authority in deadly fashion. If you find yourself in such a situation, do not protest in any way, or lower your hands – this could get you killed. Do not attempt to reach for your cell phone and start recording the event – the police will claim over your bullet-riddled corpse they thought you were reaching for a weapon.

If your roommate at college has a drug habit, definitely get a new roommate. In a moment of desperation, he can claim the drugs in the dorm belonged to you. Now you're the one in hot water, assuming the police believe him. Remove yourself from the problem, and don't wait on the residence hall assistants to do it for you.

Never touch a police officer, even he extends his hand for a handshake. Merely touching a police officer is a felony assault charge, and will get you blacklisted from any decent job in the engineering field. Never touch a cop for any reason, even if he is wantonly violating your rights. Any sort of physical resistance can get you beaten up, shot, or facing felony charges. You can always file a complaint afterward, or file a lawsuit if a lawyer thinks you have a case.

College-related events with alcohol are cop magnets. Cops love to go to such places, because they can bust underage kids for drinking, bust them for having fake IDs, bust adults for buying the alcohol for them, and probably bust a few people for weed too. Also, drunks are stupid, belligerent, and prone to fighting and acting out in public. This makes them easy marks for getting locked up. This is just another good reason to avoid being intoxicated or around idiots that are.

If you get pulled over, always make your hands visible to the officer by placing your palms on the steering wheel. Police officers become nervous and angry with people who try to conceal their hands from them. Never argue with an officer over a speeding ticket – the cost of the ticket is not worth the potential career damage of getting arrested on a much greater charge. Police are nosy during traffic stops, and a dirty car perks up their bunny ears. Keep your car clean, and keep your items out of sight and in the trunk.

If you find yourself working as a teaching assistant or tutor for a class and are male, never allow yourself to be alone with a female student. This situation makes it easy for her to claim, "Joe touched me," or "Fred said dirty words to me." Do your tutoring in a quiet yet public place, such as the library. This may seem like paranoia, but it's simply good legal defensive practice.

Always try to dismiss yourself from police encounters. Most encounters with the police are voluntary, which by definition, means they don't have to happen. Continue to dismiss yourself from the police encounter – there is no penalty for asking. If the officer says you cannot leave, then you can safely assume you are being detained, and should start saying the magic words. You do not need to wait for the officer to read you the Miranda warning before you begin exercising your rights.

11.5 Victory Through Avoidance

"Be extremely subtle, even to the point of formlessness. Be extremely mysterious, even to the point of soundlessness. Thereby you can be the director of the opponent's fate."

-Sun Tzu, *The Art of War*

An important takeaway from this chapter is that the police are not

"Officer Friendly" anymore. Police officers have enormous powers, and enjoy strong legal protections in the execution of their duties. Trying to get a cop fired or sue a police department is a fool's errand. Furthermore, police officers are paid and promoted on the basis of making arrests, and they don't care how morally upright or hardworking of a person you are. Their career advancement revolves around locking you up, and they're very good at their jobs.

The reader might suspect I have some sort of ax to grind against the police, but they would be mistaken. Cops are typically not interested in locking up science nerds like you and me. I personally have never had any negative interactions with the police, and have only been pulled over once for a busted headlight. Part of the reason I have never had a bad experience with the police is that I am generally a law-abiding person. The other reason is that I do my best to avoid places and situations likely to attract them.

If you actually need the police's help, you should probably call them. However, if you do not need their help, you should strive to avoid them as much as possible. It's just common sense that cops can't arrest you if they can't see you. Avoid areas where the police are likely to be. Don't talk to them or try to make pleasant conversation. Avoid being out late at night, as night time is when criminals and the police are most active. Remember the magic words, and this one simple rule: When they show up, the party's over. Get up out of your chair. It's time to go.

12 Getting a Job

12.1 Being Apart from the Pack

"I don't care what anyone says. Being rich is a good thing."

-Mark Cuban

The goal of engineering school is not to pointlessly torture yourself for at least four years. The goal is to use the degree as a springboard for getting a high-paying job. Getting a job might seem like a daunting task, but a degree in chemical engineering clearly separates you from the pack of applicants. The more prestigious your school, and the higher your GPA, the better the job you'll likely be able to obtain. The primary barriers to getting a job have nothing to do with your choice of degree. The primary barriers to getting any job are:

- Dropping out of high school

- Having a felony(s)

- Failing to pass a drug test

- Depending on the job, having a DUI

Depressing thought: there are people alive that have done all four of these things! If you can pass this sieve, you've already put yourself ahead of a huge chunk of the job-seeking population. Having your degree only separates you further. As an example, during the Midwest oil boom back in 2010-2015, oil companies were rejecting 50-75% of all applicants for oilfield jobs simply because so many of them had criminal records or failed the mandatory drug test [77].

12.2 The Job Search and Résumés

"Ask and it will be given to you; seek and you will find; knock and the door will be opened to you."

-The New Testament, Matthew 7:7

As discussed in section 2.4, chemical engineers get all sorts of jobs. The types of jobs you'll be applying to will probably vary greatly. Some chemical engineers go straight into the traditional process industries (e.g. petroleum refining, consumer products, and chemicals manufacture). Some pursue an MBA and go the managerial track. Some go on to law school and become patent attorneys. Others go into the consulting field, and work for a consulting firm. A small number go on to medical school. Those who pursue a PhD can enter fields far removed from the process industries. One fellow I knew at Purdue did work on supply chain management for the petroleum industry, but he was later picked up by Intel. Other members of his research group had similar projects, but were picked up by companies like Amazon to do optimization work.

It is wise to be broad in your job search. Do not be discouraged by the large number of applications you must send out. This is perfectly normal. I applied to hundreds of jobs and had multiple phone and webcam interviews before I finally got some offers. Companies often have very specific requirements for the kind of skills they want to hire someone for, and so most applicants are rejected no matter how impressive their background is. Whenever you are being considered for employment at a job, your potential employer is analyzing you in terms of an investment. Based on your education, experience level, track record, and the salary being offered, will you pay off as an investment? If not, you will likely be passed over for the job. If the hiring manager thinks you are likely to payoff, then you've got a good chance of getting it.

There are many avenues to searching for a job. Go to career fairs and hob nob. Bring copies of your resume – though have someone else look at it first. Dress up for the occasion. If you need to, buy yourself a suit. Wear a tie, dress shirt, and dress shoes. Ill-fitting dress shoes are foot killers, so be prepared to spend a lot on high quality dress shoes. Learn how to tie a tie. Wear dress socks. Shave or trim your beard.

Take a shower and wear deodorant. Brush, floss, and mouthwash your teeth – halitosis is a huge problem for engineers at career fairs. I've spoken to fellow students at on-campus career fairs whose breath smelled like a dead animal was lodged in the back of their throat. Bring a folder to hold business cards, paper to jot down any notes, multiple copies of your resume, and a map of the career fair.

PhD students will probably not have much success at career fairs, as doctoral students are expensive for employers to hire. I was told repeatedly to just apply on the company website. I joked with the recruiters about which was worse to have on your resume: a felony conviction or a PhD? By the way the recruiters at the career fairs responded when I mentioned I was a PhD student, you'd think I had done time in prison for burning down an orphanage. The only recruitment events I had reasonable success at were the specially-designated doctoral student career events, where employers were coming specifically to hire PhD students.

Most job searching is done using the internet. This can be an extremely time-consuming process, but it ought to be treated as a full-time job if you are currently unemployed. Employers can take three to four months or longer to respond to a job application, so it is unwise to apply to only a handful of jobs and hope to land one of them. Apply, apply, apply. Get a professional-sounding email address to handle correspondence with employers; you are not going to be taken seriously when you put a silly, anonymous email address down on the application. Your name will do just fine (e.g. john.smith@gmail.com). Avoid using your academic email address, since it will become defunct after you graduate. Create a unique folder for each job you apply to on your computer, and put the specific cover letter you wrote for that job into that folder. This is so you can remember what you said to the employer if they respond. Employers take forever to respond, so apply early and in great volume. I applied for jobs in the fall of 2014 and was getting rejection notices up to twelve months after I had stopped my job search. I advise writing a "canned" cover letter with a basic introduction and benediction, but then filling in that cover letter with details relevant to your experience and the specific job requirements. Put in the computer folder any other relevant documents you submitted with the application.

Résumés are in a state of flux. While it is perfectly advisable to have a paper résumé ready-to-go on your computer, many of the employers I applied to simply went to my LinkedIn page. The LinkedIn profile provided the exact same details outlined in my résumé. This trend might continue into the future, where LinkedIn, or some other competitor, takes over the résumé-posting business. Do not put a "selfie" as your LinkedIn picture. Get one of your friends to take a real picture of you wearing your dress clothes. Keep your résumé up-to-date and no more than two pages. It can become extremely exhausting writing the same information again and again into application forms, so I again recommend the LastPass software plug-in. LastPass has an extremely useful "fill forms" feature, that will automatically detect a form on a webpage and fill it in with commonly asked for information, such as your name, address, telephone number, and email address. It's a real time saver.

12.3   The Interview Process and How to Prepare for It

"The healthy man does not torture others – generally it is the tortured who turn into torturers."

-Carl Jung

Prestigious companies are extremely strict on hiring, and go to great lengths to screen poor candidates out early in the process. The interview process is a gradual escalation of interview intensity and cost on the part of the employer. Typically the first round of interviews are done via inexpensive email or phone interviews. Gradually, an examination of some type may be given electronically over the internet, followed up by a webcam interview. The final phase is a face-to-face interview on location and a tour of the workplace facilities. Doctoral-level job candidates can expect to give a presentation on their graduate research to the interviewers, and must be able to answer any questions they ask.

Every company does interviews differently. At Epic Systems, I had several phone interviews, a psychological exam, and an IQ test that was electronically proctored through my webcam. At BASF, the interview process first began as a phone interview, and then proceeded to a webcam-based video interview. Colleagues of mine explained the interview process at a large petroleum company. The interview involved a group collaboration on a given engineering problem, with the interviewers examining the problem-solving strategies and leadership skills of the various group members. At my current job, I had multiple phone interviews with my future co-workers, and then was flown up to Milwaukee for several rounds of face-to-face interviews. Some job interviewers will ask you the same questions over and over again, to see if you are keeping your story straight – somewhat like a police interrogation.

A good idea to prepare for any interview is to study up on various questions that are commonly pitched during job interviews. There are too many questions to write about in this book, but there are many sources on the internet (especially Glassdoor.com) that will discuss the specific interview questions asked by employers at a specific company. Be mindful of what kind of job you are interviewing for. If you are interviewing for a research and development position, you will want to be able to discuss any research you did, either as an undergraduate student or a graduate. If you are entering a more traditional process industry job, you will want to be able to discuss any internships you held and what you did during that internship.

It is wise to be honest during a job interview, since any hint of skulduggery will get your application trashed immediately. During my phone interviews, I was repeatedly asked, "Do you have skill A? Have you ever worked with B? Can you do C?" The answer was usually "No," except for a few skills I actually did have and answered "Yes" to. If you are asked such questions, do not lie and claim to be an expert at every skill the interviewer questions you about. No one is a master at everything; they will merely assume you're telling them what they want to hear. Do not project weakness or nervousness; the company wants to feel they are getting someone who is confident in their skills.

The interviewer might ask some curve ball questions to try and throw you off balance, but try to think the question through step-by-step before responding, and do not take offense. Always try to use concrete examples from your schooling to demonstrate that you have a particular skill. For example, if the interviewer were to ask you, "How are your writing and communication skills?" any moron would reply, "Oh, they're great," without any evidence to support their claim. Instead, refer the interviewer to any published work you have, or projects you wrote up for a course. Some schools require a senior thesis, which could also be a good demonstration of your writing skills. And likewise for any other question referring to your experiences and skills, whether it is leadership or technical skills.

You should prepare your own list of questions to grill the inter-

viewer with. Relevant questions include what projects are being offered, what the work space looks like, what the work hour expectations
are, whether the company has the tools available to do the kind of
work you are expected to do, how much travel is required, if the team
members are "nice people," has anyone lately left the company and
why, who the major competitors are, and whether the surrounding area
is safe. Do your homework on the area surrounding the work site,
much like when you were researching the area surrounding your university. Is there a crime a problem? Have there been shootings or mug-
gings of employees? Will your car be safe in the parking lot? Will you
even need a car? Will there be a long commute? Where do your future
co-workers live? It is an extremely bad idea to come to a job interview
and not have any questions to ask the interviewers, as it presents a lack
of interest in the job and a lack of self-direction. Do not bring up salary
at the job interview.

Another wise question to ask your interviewers and future co-
workers is "How long have you worked here?" If the answer is consistently, "a couple of years," that might set off alarm bells. Well-run companies are strict on hiring, but do their best to hang on to good employees. Poorly-run companies hire on lots of people to meet an up-
surge of demand and then fire everyone when the work is done. It
could also be a sign of high employee turnover, which could be due to
any number of bad reasons. Consistently demanding long hours will
cause many people to leave after a few years. The workplace might also
be unbearable for people. It's a good sign when people have worked
for many years at the same company. It shows you can have a long,
productive career with them if you do your job effectively.

Control your big mouth during the job interview. Do not reveal
details about your life that are not relevant to the job or living in the
nearby area. Don't talk about your wife or girlfriend, or if you plan on
having children soon. Don't bring up religion or sexual orientation.
These things have nothing to do with the job, and can only be used
against you. Do not talk about any big debts you have or major pur-
chases you are planning, as this can be used as leverage against you to
lowball your salary – your employer figures, "Hey this guy needs the
money." Avoid speaking negatively about your previous employers
and co-workers, since this makes you seem hard to get along with.

12.4   The Usefulness of Internships

"Indeed, this very exorbitance of profit shows, that the industry of the master is paid out of all proportion with that of the slave."

-Jean-Baptiste Say

From what I have observed, it is difficult to get a job straight out of engineering school as a direct-hire. Companies are risk-averse to spending money on someone who has not been proven yet. A way to get your foot in the door is an undergraduate internship, where you go to work at a company for a lower wage but gain valuable experience you can put on your resume. If you get an internship, I will put you on notice: do the absolute best job you can. Even if you decide not to pursue full-time employment with that company, your boss can be an especially persuasive reference in the future. Other companies will hire engineers as contractors for a specified period of time, and then decide afterward whether to offer full-time employment. I personally never did an internship, though several of my friends have, and they paid off handsomely.

12.5   What Employers Should Be Offering You

"A good job is more than just a paycheck. A good job fosters independence and discipline, and contributes to the health of the community. A good job is a means to provide for the health and welfare of your family, to own a home, and save for retirement."

-James H. Douglas, Jr.

Do not pursue any job that requires you to pay for travel and airfare expenses to come to the interview. I had one outfit try to pull that on me, and I didn't follow up with that position. A company that cannot afford basic human resources costs is probably not long for this world. Also, never blindly take unsolicited job offers, since a company that will hire anyone probably sucks. Avoid job postings that post salary information up front; bringing up salary information early is like discussing sex on the first date.

It is generally expected that your travel, lodging, and food expenses will be paid for when you are heading to a job interview. Competitive salary ranges depend on the particular industry, the prestige of your university, and your GPA. Definitely do your homework to get some idea as to what salary you should be getting offered, as the internet is replete with salary information by region and industry. A good job offer will offer a competitive starting salary, full medical benefits, and usually some kind of profit-sharing incentive – either stock options, or a retirement matching program.

Salary negotiation is a tough business, and is probably the most difficult part of a job interview process. If you ask for too high of a starting salary, you'll lose the job offer completely. Ask too low and you'll be short-changing yourself. Some companies (e.g. the oil companies) offer high but non-negotiable salaries. You can put yourself in a stronger negotiating position by having multiple competing offers. That way, if you overshoot on one of the offers and lose it, you'll still have several others you can rely on. Competitive bidding between two or more employers is precisely the sort of situation that your potential employers will try to avoid, but is immensely favorable to you.

If you accept the job offer, it should be expected that the company will pay for all moving expenses and reimburse most expenses paid during the move. Some companies are quite generous in this regard, and will go to great lengths to make your move comfortable. Among other things, they will help you sell your house, find a new home, and help you get a new mortgage, as well as paying for all of your hotel expenses during the interim while you have no place to live. To reiterate, a friend of mine from graduate school lived in a great hotel with his family for thirty days while he and his wife hunted for a new home. The oil company footed the entire bill. If a drug screen is required, the company should pay for that completely.

12.6 Soft Skills that can Increase Your Marketability

"He that is kind is free, though he is a slave; he that is evil is a slave, though he be a king."

-St. Augustine of Hippo

Being a nice guy or polite young lady can go a long way to scoring a job, so present yourself as a nice, collegial person at the job interview.

This really just requires a bit of common sense. Dress appropriately and act politely. If you are treated to lunch or dinner by the employer, eat like a civilized human and don't talk with your mouth full. A common rule I have heard is to "never order the most expensive thing on the menu," but I am skeptical as to how big of a deal this really is. I have been to professional dinners where the host ordered far more food than I did, and more expensive dishes as well. Furthermore, they are usually using the corporate credit card, so it should not matter to them what you order anyways – it's the company's money, not their own. If the most expensive dish is wildly expensive, then avoid it, but if the price gap between the next-most-expensive dish is only a few bucks, you're probably in the clear. Be cautious with alcohol during a lunch or dinner interview, since alcohol lowers your inhibitions and is a truth serum. Always remain in control of your senses during an interview or dinner. I advise abstaining from alcohol during any type of employment interview or professional dinner.

Knowing a foreign language can be a serious boon to getting a good job, especially if you are keen on foreign travel. Knowing a smattering of words and phrases from high school German doesn't count. You'll need a professional-level competency to have value added. It would take an econometrician to tell you which language provides the most payoff, but this sort of analysis in my opinion isn't amenable to dollars-and-cents. Is there a place in the world outside of your home country where you would prefer to live and work? If that is China, learn Mandarin Chinese. If Japan, learn Japanese. Knowing a foreign language can position you to act as a liaison for a major company trying to do business overseas.

On the subject of languages, foreign-born Indian and Chinese students tend to lack good spoken English skills. This can disadvantage them during a job search during interviews. If you cannot express yourself intelligibly, you hurt your chances of getting the job. No one wants to work with people they must struggle to understand, especially in a field like engineering, where solid communication of complex ideas is critical to success. If English is not your first language, I suggest getting some audio books spoken by a native American-English speaker and speak along with the narrator. Practice, practice, practice your speaking until you can sound like an American. Read out loud to an audiobook with the actual text in your hand. After a while of doing this, your ability to speak English will dramatically improve.

12.7 Other Things to Consider When Deciding Whether or Not to Take a Job

"God gave us the gift of life; it is up to us to give ourselves the gift of living well."

-Voltaire

Quality of life can be a problem as a chemical engineer in the process industries. For public safety reasons, chemical plants are usually situated out in the boonies. My friend "Marcus" landed his first job with a prestigious Fortune 500 company ... which had him living for over five years in the middle of nowhere in Louisiana. It was pretty rough on him. While the pay was great, the town he lived in was miserable. Towns near chemical plants are often wracked by Latin American-style wealth inequality – the people that work at the plant have plenty of disposable income, and everyone else is broke. As a single male, Marcus lived a monk-like existence during those five years. Virtually every female in town had a serious weight problem, worked a menial retail job, and/or was a single mom. None of the young women in town had anything going for them in life, except to potentially nab one of the plant employees to serve as a meal ticket. It must have been especially hard on Marcus. He had just left USF, where beautiful women were a dime-a-dozen, and he had a steady girlfriend. Now he was in a place where there were virtually no beautiful women to be found.

Since the town was stuck in the middle of nowhere in the South, all people did for fun was eat "good old southern home-style cooking" – the kind of garbage food that clogs your arteries and quickly packs on the pounds: fried chicken, fried gator tail, hush puppies, corn bread, bacon-bit mashed potatoes – food that's been fried in lard, fat, and butter. Most of the plant employees had serious weight problems, too.

The situation is similar elsewhere. I investigated working for a particular defense company based out in the Midwest. At Purdue, they gave a detailed seminar presentation on how they were looking to expand. They wanted people to help build new rocket engines out in the middle of nowhere in Utah. For hundreds of miles there is literally nothing around you. The seminar speaker continually reminded us of the "beautiful scenery" that Utah had to offer. I sure hope it is beautiful, because you'd be seeing a lot of it. A professor I spoke to at a professional dinner told me that his first job out of college was based in rural West Virginia, where a constant problem was local hillbillies taking potshots at the large chemical storage tanks with their shotguns.

Other kinds of engineers do not have this kind of problem, mainly because they don't work on things that go boom. Car factories typically don't explode, so electrical, electronics, and mechanical engineers can work in factories in nice urban settings, with plenty of activities and night life to offer a young person. Likewise with electrical engineers, who mainly design circuits and widgets with minimal public safety hazards.

Working in a chemical plant can also be filthy, smelly work. During my youth, my mother would drive my brother and me up to Indiana to see our grandma. Our drive passed through Perry, Florida, where at one point there was a paper factory. We never caught sight of the paper factory, but we sure did smell it. It was one of the most putrid smells I've ever gotten a whiff of – though I have never smelled a skunk, which I'm told is still worse. The situation is not much better for petroleum engineers, who not only must endure filthy, dangerous work, but work long hours on top of it.

The weather can also be a big problem. I love the Florida weather, and miss it greatly. A problem though, is that there is virtually no work for a PhD chemical engineer in Florida outside of the university system. Despite my best efforts, the only places I could find work with my qualifications were places that get cold in the wintertime. Other engineering specialties don't have this problem. You can work in a much wider variety of locales, even if there is a modest pay hit. Though I will admit, some of my friends from Purdue were able to land jobs in Houston, Texas, where the weather is much more mild than Wisconsin.

I advise the reader to carefully weigh what their options will be with the end game in mind. A major task, which only you can do for yourself, is to research as many different companies and jobs as possible. What kind of job do you want? Which courses do you enjoy the most? Do you want to teach? Do you want to go more of a technical track or get more into project management? All of these questions will require some thought and introspection on your part in order to find the answers. While the oil and pharmaceutical companies typically offer top pay, it is generally a poor idea to base your ideal job solely on the basis of starting salary. Job satisfaction is far more important, as a high-paying miserable job will slowly take its toll on your health and sanity. Bear in mind the location of where you'll be working. If you hate the cold, try to avoid working where there are harsh winters. If you're a city slicker, you might not be happy in a rural area.

13 Chemical Engineering Versus Medical School

13.1 A Comparison Between the Subjects

"Come now, and let us reason together..."

-The Old Testament, Isaiah 1:18

If you are smart enough to get through chemical engineering, you are probably smart enough to be a doctor – in fact, a great doctor. There are many altruistic reasons for becoming a doctor. Love of one's fellow man, pity for the sick and wounded, and concern for the welfare of children are common reasons for becoming a doctor. High social status is another reason. And of course, there's also the money factor, which is the focus of this chapter.

Financially, however, the medical profession is a big loser.

"How can that be?" you may ask. "Don't doctors make tons of money?" It's true that physicians earn high incomes. A doctor in a hot specialty, in his prime earning years, can clear a million dollars a year in gross salary earnings. But all is not well in Camelot.

The purpose of this chapter is not to smear or besmirch the practice of medicine, or denigrate physicians. The purpose is to expose extraordinarily bright people to an alternate career path, that is significantly less risky, generates a comfortable income, and is just as intellectually rewarding as medicine. Throughout my undergraduate education, I saw intelligent, energetic people subjecting themselves to brutal, cutthroat competition to get into medical school, punishing themselves with endless memorization tasks, and falsely believing that medicine was the only way to earn a good living. It doesn't have to be that way.

The practice of medicine is not the only way to help the sick and afflicted. A chemical or biomedical engineer can have a far greater impact on the lives of far more people by developing new treatments that beat the current state-of-the-art. Biomedical engineers invent new ways of doing surgery, new tools, and new therapies that can help legions more people than a single surgeon can over the course of his career.

And they can make a fortune doing it.

If you truly believe medicine to be your calling in life, then by all means, pursue it. My goal is just to give you pertinent facts, so you don't make a decision operating under the false assumption that studying medicine automatically leads to wealth. Chemical engineering could still be a wise choice of undergraduate degree in this case, since a chemical engineering degree is far more valuable than the "biomedical sciences" degrees that are commonly acquired by pre-medical students. If you decide after four years of chemical engineering that you no longer want to pursue medicine, you can still get a great job elsewhere. If you decide to pursue the study of medicine, you will find – with a high GPA – that medical schools are particularly keen on recruiting engineers [78]. Successful engineering students have proven themselves able to think fast and accurately under pressure – two big qualities that make a good physician.

13.2   Medical Doctors, Taxes, and the Difference Between "Income" and "Wealth"

"Annual income twenty pounds, annual expenditure nineteen six, result happiness. Annual income twenty pounds, annual expenditure twenty pound ought and six, result misery."

-Charles Dickens, *David Copperfield*

The definitions of "income" and "wealth" are crisp and distinct, but people often confuse them. Income is the amount of money flowing into your bank account within a given time period. It can come from many sources, such as income generated from investments, from the sale of property, royalties, as a bill for services rendered, or most commonly, from a paycheck. We typically assess incomes in terms of annual earnings (e.g. $75,000 per year). The money you earn from a paycheck is one of the worst ways to earn income in America, due to the confiscatory tax system that punishes people with high incomes. Physicians earn extremely high incomes, which makes them prime meat for the Internal Revenue Service. A doctor earning $200,000 per year – as of this writing in 2016 – can expect to pay over $47,000 in federal income taxes. Nearly three months out of the year you're not working for you, for your patients, or for the hospital – you're working for the federal government.

Wealth is synonymous with "net worth." Net worth is the total sum of all of your assets (e.g. investment portfolio, cash, oil and mineral rights, real estate, etc.) minus the sum of all of your liabilities. It is possible for someone with a low income to become wealthy through wise investments and frugality. It is also possible for someone with a huge income to be living paycheck-to-paycheck due to riotous living and unrestrained spending.

People with high incomes and low net worth are epidemic in American society. For instance, professional athletes are some of the most obvious offenders, earning multi-million dollar contracts but finding themselves flat broke within five years of retirement due to extravagant lifestyles and having too many children. Physicians are another huge offender, as they typically do not accumulate wealth commensurate with their age and incomes [26].

In addition to the aforementioned high tax burden, there are several reasons for this high-income-low-wealth paradox among physicians,. For one, physicians require lengthy educations, during which they are not earning any income, have no investment portfolio, and are taking on enormous amounts of debt to attend undergraduate college and medical school (we assume no scholarship or fellowship support).

Also, physicians must pay a fortune every year in malpractice insurance. I sat next to an anesthesiologist on a plane once, and without batting an eye, he told me his family could live off what he pays in malpractice insurance every year. Decide to not pay malpractice insurance? One lawsuit can wipe out everything you have earned for yourself.

Physicians – for whatever reasons – seem attracted to high-consumption lifestyles. They like to drive luxury cars, marry – and divorce – fancy women, live in big houses in exclusive neighborhoods, and send their children to the finest private schools. While I lack hard evidence for this conjecture, I theorize that despite their high intelligence and thorough educations, regular interaction with death causes physicians to value "living for the moment." When you live for the moment, long-range financial planning doesn't make any sense. They may also be consumption-oriented due to the Spartan existence they endured while in medical school and during their residency. Whatever the reasons for this hyper-consumption, the end effect is the same: all of this spending leaves little left over for saving and investments.

To reiterate, our government is poor at targeting wealthy people for taxation but is excellent at targeting high income earners. People who invest heavily into tax-sheltered investments tend to realize a much lower percentage of their wealth in annual taxes. The key to becoming wealthy is early, consistent investment into sound holdings, and to take advantage of tax-privileged investments whenever possible.

13.3   The Downsides of Being a Medical Doctor

"He's a fool that makes his doctor his heir."

-Benjamin Franklin

The psychological aspect of being a doctor, especially an emergency room physician or surgeon, cannot be overstated. As a medical doctor, despite your most valiant efforts, patients will die in front of you. People can be horribly mangled in car and motorcycle accidents, or grotesquely disfigured from burn trauma. Obstetricians deliver stillborn babies. Oncologists are sometimes little more than painkiller dispensers for dying cancer patients. While anything is possible, it is unlikely a chemical or biomedical engineer will have to deal with such mental trauma.

Doctors have an extraordinarily arduous educational track that requires the doctor-hopeful to saddle themselves with enormous amounts of debt and assume the huge risk, in terms of time and money, that they will actually be able to obtain the medical degree and start making real money. The track is approximately as follows:

- four years of undergraduate study

- four years of basic medical studies in medical school

- Up to seven years of residency ("Residency" is a period of wage slavery for doctors)

In total, the hapless pre-medical student is staring down up to fifteen years of higher education before they can finally practice medicine on their own and finally start cranking in the big bucks.

This educational track is also extremely risky, as there is no prize for second-place: you have to go all the way to the end of this enormous education or you get nothing. If you decide halfway through medical school that medicine is not for you, guess what? You can't be a doctor. And are stuck with two years of medical school debt, plus whatever you owe from your undergraduate years. Good luck earning the money needed to pay those bills off. With only undergraduate pre-med qualifications, the most you can do usually is teach high school science classes.

The debt level doctors must take on is out of sight. Typical undergraduate debt is about $35,000, while typical medical school debt is about $300,000. Even with high incomes, physicians can struggle for years to pay off such an enormous debt. Assuming a 6% interest rate, the physician must pay at least $18,000 per year just to neutralize the interest accrual, and that doesn't even scratch the principal! If they decide to join a practice, they have to "buy in" to the practice, which can cost tens of thousands of dollars. The debt just keeps piling up.

Doctors are actually underpaid when one factors in the crippling hours they have to work. Doctors can be forced to work up to sixteen-hour shifts, and do not get overtime. Despite owning lots of toys, there is often little time to enjoy any of them. Family life can suffer, and marriages can be strained to the breaking point due to such long work hours. Your children will be grown up before you even know it.

13.4 Chemical Engineering as an Alternative to Pre-Med

"Isn't it a bit unnerving that doctors call what they do 'practice?'"

-George Carlin

If you are unswayed by the previous sections, and are still willing to go through with becoming a physician, I nonetheless encourage you to choose chemical engineering. Chemical engineering is a far more marketable undergraduate degree than "biomedical sciences", biology, biochemistry, or microbiology. You can complete the necessary pre-medicine requirements with a few extra classes, and your degree will be much more persuasive to the medical schools. Also, chemical engineering is a powerful hedge in case you decide medical school is not for you. If you pursue a strictly pre-med degree and decide after four years that you no longer want to be a doctor, you're left with a crappy degree. If you major in chemical engineering, you will be left with a much more marketable degree.

14 Chemical Engineering and Entrepreneurship

14.1 The Road Less Traveled

"It's hard to beat a person who never gives up."

-Babe Ruth

Entrepreneurship is a forgotten choice for many young men in America – mainly because it is simply not spoken of in the media except for sensationalized dramatizations like *Shark Tank*, not discussed in the schools, and the overwhelming emphasis of school anyways is on securing a job on the corporate plantation. However, entrepreneurship is an excellent pathway for intelligent, self-disciplined people who desire the freedom to direct their own work.

Most people think they are not brilliant enough to become entrepreneurs, but this misidentifies the problem. Many entrepreneurs do not have very original business ideas to start with. There were already computer companies before Steve Jobs and Michael Dell. There were already operating systems before Bill Gates and Steve Wozniak. Jeff Bezos sold books over the internet. Peter Thiel merely started another investment fund. Entrepreneurs are people who are comfortable with taking risks; that is, risking their time and money on enterprises that are not guaranteed to make money and have the potential to be a total loss. People who are uncomfortable with taking risks tend to make poor entrepreneurs. People who make foolhardy bets likewise are unlikely to succeed. The happy medium is found in smart individuals who actively hunt for opportunities both with a high-payoff and a high likelihood of succeeding (and better yet, require low investment).

There's an endless supply of mundane business ideas that can be searched for on the internet. However, the biggest money is found in the commercialization of new technologies. Most of the interest is currently in technologies related to electronics, computers, and the internet, but this is only a fraction of the entire U.S. technology sector. This is where a chemical engineering education can really shine. The entrepreneur armed with a chemical engineering education has a chance at developing something truly new, which could make them as rich as a Rockefeller. Whether its inventing a revolutionary new material, applying an existing technology in an unconventional way, or changing the way an entire industry conducts business, chemical engineers have huge potential for making it in the business world.

14.2 The Drawbacks of Entrepreneurship

"If you're not a risk taker, you should get the hell out of business."

-Ray A. Kroc

The main drawback of entrepreneurship is the risk. As the manager of the business, you accept all the risk of the enterprise. If it goes belly up, you lose all of the investment you sunk into it, period. There is no prize for second place. If you can't pay your employees anymore, they will stop showing up. If you cannot pay your creditors, they'll repossess your equipment. And God help you if you cannot pay your taxes!

Entrepreneurship is a stressful career choice. There is always uncertainty about the future. With equipment malfunctioning, good employees leaving, good employees turning out to be bad employees, customers reneging on contracts, threats of lawsuits, politicians raising your taxes, and being displaced by competitors, entrepreneurship places far more stressors upon you than working an ordinary job. Most businesses do not succeed to long-term profitability or are offered a buyout.

Things can also be rough starting up, since you will be shorthanded on people with high-quality skills. You'll have to oversee all of the key aspects of the business: marketing, getting the work done, finding customers, keeping customers happy, keeping tabs on competitors, maintaining good relations with suppliers, accounting, paying off the government, attending to clients, answering the phone, and a host of other activities. Getting quality people is a continual battle for the startup, and keeping good people requires a peaceful work environment, good benefits, and competitive pay.

While it is up to you to set your work schedule, successful entrepreneurs often work more than the standard forty-hour work week –

often over eighty hours a week. This stress can keep up for years before the business finally becomes profitable and you can finally look into flipping the business or hiring full-time professional staff to take on most of the management responsibilities.

14.3   The Benefits of Entrepreneurship

"There aren't many downsides to being rich, other than paying taxes and having relatives asking for money."

-Bill Murray

Despite the drawbacks of entrepreneurship, it has significant upsides.

For one, you are your own boss, and therefore it is impossible to fire you; only you can fire you. You are the CEO, answerable only to God Almighty himself. As an entrepreneur, you have unlimited freedom in directing the course of your work. If you have more work than you can handle, you simply delegate some of it to one of your employees. If they are swamped, it's time to hire a new employee to take the weight off your shoulders. Furthermore, you have complete control over your schedule. If you want to take a day off, you don't have to call in and beg or play hooky. You just take the day off, no problem at all! Do you do your best work at night and prefer to sleep during the day? A regular job would never accept that, but with entrepreneurship it's a snap. If you're in an industry amenable to telecommuting, you don't even need to leave the house and commute on a cold morning, no permission required.

As the CEO, you get to determine how the affairs of your enterprise are conducted. If you ever wondered at your job, "Why are we doing it this way? It would be so much more efficient doing it another way," but felt powerless to change things, then entrepreneurship might be for you. If you spot inefficiency, you resolve to fix it immediately. If you see an employee struggling, you try to get the resources together to help them out – whether its more training, shifting their workload around, or firing them and getting someone better.

As an entrepreneur, you never have to hunt for a job or go through some moronic job interview. You simply get a business license, and pay a lawyer a modest fee to set your corporation up for you, and prest-o-change-o! You're in business!

You have unlimited freedom in choosing who you want to work with, and who you no longer want to work with. If someone is behaving in a way you find disagreeable, you simply fire them, or sever your business ties. I find this to be one of the most tempting upsides to being an entrepreneur, as I've had to deal with many people I would never have worked with voluntarily given the choice.

Another huge bonus to entrepreneurship is that there are no formal educational, experience, or professional requirements. High school diploma? No problem. Bachelor's in Chemical Engineering? You're in there! Doctorate? Even better! While extra education is always helpful, it is not required. I will hedge a bit here though, and admit that most entrepreneurs do have college degrees, and many successful entrepreneurs were excellent students (e.g. Jeff Bezos). Also, higher education credentials add clout, and can make it easier to get investment capital.

Probably the biggest bonus though to entrepreneurship though is the money. As an engineer, you can expect your end-of-career pay to be around $120,000 – maybe more, maybe less. Entrepreneurs have no theoretical limit to their potential earnings. If you invent and patent something that suddenly everyone can't live without, your grandchildren's grandchildren will be set for life. Most millionaires in America became millionaires through ownership of their own business [26]. The wealthiest and most powerful people in the country are business owners: Jeff Bezos, Michael Dell, Bill Gates, the late Steve Jobs, Phil Knight, Peter Thiel, Sergey Brin, Larry Page, and Mark Zuckerberg all made their personal fortunes through entrepreneurship.

14.4 Getting Involved In College, Patents, and Acquiring Capital

"The critical ingredient is getting off your butt and doing something. It's as simple as that. A lot of people have ideas, but there are few who decide to do something about them now. Not tomorrow. Not next week. But today. The true entrepreneur is a doer, not a dreamer."

-Nolan Bushnell

For starters, I would get some books on entrepreneurship and accounting that go into far more detail than this book does (*Entrepreneur Magazine* publishes a good starting book [79]). Books on accounting, taxes, and the legal aspects of running a business are also wise investments. More specific books on entrepreneurship in the high-tech sector can also be sources of wisdom. Books in general will likely be a key part of your life as an entrepreneur, since it pays to be well-informed.

Some universities (e.g. Stanford University) have worked hard to foster a culture of technology entrepreneurship on their campuses. Some universities have their own venture capital funds that only alumni are allowed to invest in, and are used to fund startups on the campus [80]. Purdue University had an Entrepreneurship Club, and an entire section of the campus dedicated to technology entrepreneurship. Getting involved on campus with entrepreneurial organizations and building connections is a good starting point. Kick around ideas, and don't be too worried about someone "stealing" your brilliant idea. It's one thing to have an idea, but entirely another thing to bring it to reality and observe profitability. Ask questions, learn about the technology someone is proposing. Think up your own ideas, whether it's a smart phone app, a new device, or a new material, and bounce those ideas off your friends. If you come up with something you cannot readily punch any holes in, it might be time to escalate and start brainstorming a business plan.

A great way to get involved is to participate in entrepreneurship competitions, whether it's a "two-minute elevator pitch competition", a presentation competition, or a poster competition. These competitions can lead to significant funding and useful connections that can make your dream a reality. A friend of mine teamed up with a fellow from the business school at USF to pitch his new catalyst idea to investors and won a $50,000 competition. Bigger competitions can lead to even more money, publicity, and connections.

It is wise to familiarize yourself with patent law, since patents are the lifeblood of the technology industry. While patents have their evils associated with them, they are necessary to secure investments. A patent is a legal document guaranteeing a temporary monopoly on the commercialization and licensing of an invention. Patents last up to twenty years, which is a decent window of time to recoup investments and generate a profit on the technology. Royalties from licensing are another avenue of approach if you don't think it's worth it to build a business around the patent. Patents are expensive however; it costs around $50,000 to obtain a patent. That might sound like a great deal of money, but it is a necessary evil. No investor will give you the time of day if you try to enter the technology sector without a patent, or portfolio of patents, on your technology.

Work on your writing and speaking skills. You will need to write a business plan eventually to pitch to investors, and if you come off sounding like a complete imbecile, your odds of acquiring capital plummet. This is probably one of the toughest skills for engineers to master; most engineers I know absolutely detest writing. Unfortunately, no one is going to give you any money if you cannot concisely and accurately convey to them what your ideas and intentions are regarding the structure and operation of the business. Investors aren't stupid. They know most problems with troubled companies lie with ineffective, idiotic management. Investors have less-risky options than your business, and you need to be offering a significant risk premium in order to convince them to invest in you. Always be honest in your writings and deeds. If you get a reputation for dishonesty, you will find it very difficult to get funding. No one wants to work with – much less give money to – a scoundrel.

15 Concluding Remarks, Final Perspective, and Further Reading

"The starting point of all achievement is desire."

-Napoleon Hill

That's it, my friend, that's all I have to say. If you decide that all of this math and science stuff isn't very fun, then don't worry about it. Chemical engineering is not for everybody. Perhaps there are other fields of engineering that interest you – but I'll warn you ahead of time: they are still going to be mathematically demanding. Beyond what I have already written, I've also provided two chapters in the appendix: one on future technologies in chemical engineering, and the other on process systems engineering. The first is to give the reader an idea of what sorts of technologies are on the horizon. The second is to give the reader an idea of the sorts of things I work on at my job.

The references in this book, except for the textbooks, were found freely on the Internet, and not behind paywalls. The reader is encouraged to peruse the bibliography for further reading material. Government and professional bodies are good sources for employment prospects – especially the Bureau of Labor Statistics and the American Institute of Chemical Engineers. Google Scholar is a treasure trove of published academic papers related to chemical engineering. While you probably won't understand much of what you read in these papers, they will give you a good idea as to what sorts of technologies are being researched presently, and what lies on the horizon.

Before committing an enormous amount of time, money, and labor to getting a chemical engineering degree, make sure it's what you want to do. This is not an endeavor you can half-ass and expect to succeed. If you read this book, and your interest in chemical engineering has been piqued, I would suggest you expand your research into the topic. Amazon sells older editions of engineering textbooks that you can buy for a song, and get an even better idea of what chemical engineers study. If you find these books interesting, even if you don't understand much of what you read, then chemical engineering is probably the path for you. Also, check out the AICHE website for a full list of past capstone design problems the organization has published for its annual plant design contest. And of course, get a professionally-administered IQ test – or take the SAT or AFQT and use a correlation – to see if you have the mental hardware upstairs to do chemical engineering school.

The immense amount of mathematics that accompanies the study of chemical engineering is a turn-off for many people. However, you may still be interested in getting into a technical profession. If that is the case, I suggest the reader investigate technical trades. These kinds of jobs do not require four years like engineering school, and can often be completed at lower cost in only two years. When there is a spike in demand for their specialty, skilled tradesmen can make a killing.

Preparing in high school now is the best way to ready yourself for engineering school. Get involved in the Advanced Placement program, and study yourself silly. Take AP courses relevant to chemical engineering, such as calculus, chemistry, and physics, and pass your examinations with a 4 or a 5. You might also be able to take some general education courses at the local community college, which will also help trim costs. Living at home with your parents can be a drag, but it's cheaper than living on campus at the state university. Take your studying seriously while in college, and make it your first priority – followed closely by taking care of your mental and physical health. Reward yourself after major victories and jobs-well-done. Be your own toughest critic.

In further preparation for engineering school, I strongly advise the reader to practice and strengthen their writing skills. Most engineers I know abhor writing, but being able to communicate your ideas effectively is a key skill an engineer needs to master. The only way to get better at writing is to do it. Consider keeping an encrypted private journal on your computer, and write down your thoughts about various subjects into it. Even one page a day over a long period of time will go a long way towards powering up your writing skills. Reading and writing go hand-in-hand. People who consistently read lengthy, difficult texts tend to have a broad vocabulary, and a broad vocabulary makes writing much easier. Make a habit of reading in your free time. Amazon's Kindle platform has legions of classics available for free due to being decades out of copyright. The more you read and write, the more your skills will improve.

Again, I will not wish the reader luck. As I have already stated, you are holding all the cards. Luck has nothing to do with the equation regarding your success in engineering school. The more you study, the more you are willing to sacrifice, and the longer you can endure hardship, the greater your success will be in engineering. If you love mathematics and science, and want to be at the forefront of human progress, then go for it. Pursue chemical engineering as your career and give it your all. Don't let anything stand in your way of achieving your goal of getting that degree and getting the career you want. In this world, you only have one person you can rely on and trust: you. No one can get that degree and lifestyle for you. You have to do it for yourself.

16 APPENDIX

17 Future Technologies in Chemical Engineering

17.1 Overview

"Any sufficiently advanced technology is indistinguishable from magic."

-Arthur C. Clarke

There are too many new technologies to cover in depth, so this section serves to just give a thumbnail sketch of new horizons in chemical engineering research. A challenge to writing this chapter has been that scientific literature is so often couched in unintelligible jargon as to make it unreadable. This is done partly out of laziness, because writing well is hard to do, and partly also to fulfill personal ambitions: mediocre work sounds more impressive the more jargon is concocted to describe it. For example, "in silico" is a fancy Latin phrase for "The work was done on a computer." This behavior is not unique to science. It is the same reason lawyers and physicians deal so much in obscure Latin phrases. I have done my best to "render the fat" and make this section as intelligible as possible to someone with only a high-school background. Nonetheless, a modicum of Googling might be needed to help understand some of the more technical aspects of this chapter.

17.2 Process Intensification

"Great things are done by a series of small things brought together."

-Vincent van Gogh

As a general observation, the goals of future chemical engineering technologies will be the control of matter and energy at ever-decreasing length and time scales [2], [36], [37], [81]. In fact, the arbitrary control of matter and energy at the nanoscale has attracted the attention of the highest levels of government, as well as private capital [37], [38]. New processes are also being researched for the production of chemicals.

Instead of scaling up processes, research is being done into scaling them down, where much finer control over product quality is possible. Heat and mass transfer rates are ten to a hundred times faster in miniaturized reactors and microfluidic devices versus regularly-sized equipment [36]. This research area, termed "process intensification," entails thinking up ingenious new technologies for performing industrial-scale operations with less size, less capital cost, far less equipment, and fewer processing steps [36].

17.3 Materials Science

"There's a way to do it better - find it."

-Thomas Edison

Chemical engineers are poised to have enormous impact on diverse technology fields such as biomaterials, catalysts, polymers and composites, energy storage systems, and organo-electronics [38]. Government funding is heavily targeted towards the development of new materials [37], [38]. Grand challenges include the design, synthesis, and control of new materials which are engineered down to the nanoscale. Another problem in the field of materials science is the slow development time to the commercialization of new material technologies. Currently, it can take twenty years before a new material becomes commercially viable [38]. Rapid-prototyping technologies are being investigated to remedy this situation, with the ultimate goal being able to print materials with nanometer-scale resolution [37], [38].

Composite materials are materials composed of multiple material components (e.g. a plastic layer, a metal layer, and a ceramic layer). The use of lightweight composite materials in industrial applications have been estimated to have an economic impact of over $500 billion to the US GDP [38]. Organo-electronic composite devices have a variety of applications in energy storage, medical diagnostics, and biocompatible electronics, and are estimated to be a $10 billion industry.

Polymers are found in nearly all sectors of advanced industrial economies – especially the energy, transportation, aerospace, electronics, and biotechnology sectors [38]. Currently, polymer precursors are dominated by oil-derived polyolefins, but efforts are being made to identify new feedstock materials to reduce the dependence on oil for plastics production. Technologies are being researched for converting waste carbon dioxide (CO_2) into useful polymers using solar energy [2].

The microchip industry, as of this writing, is rapidly approaching an impenetrable wall. The industry has been able to increase computation power simply by improving their ability to make transistors smaller and smaller. Eventually, however, due to the Heisenberg Uncertainty Principle and quantum tunneling, it will become impossible for transistors to function below a certain size [37]. New materials and approaches will be needed to keep computing power flowing, and chemical engineers are exactly the sort of people to whom investment will be directed to make this happen.

The data storage industry is always looking for ways to increase memory storage densities. Current hard disk storage densities are about 0.25 gigabytes/cm^2, though newer technologies on the horizon can theoretically increase this figure by six-hundred-fold [36].

Even though the growth of chemical knowledge over the past several decades has shown an exponential increase, materials engineering is still a wide-open field [36]. Now over fourteen million unique substances are known – most of which are synthetic, not found in nature. And yet even this number is minuscule compared to the number of compounds that haven't been synthesized, considering there are ninety-two naturally-occurring elements on the periodic table. There is still plenty of room for scientific (and economic...!) growth. Numerous technologies are being investigated for making better materials. Higher temperature materials would allow heat engines to run at higher efficiency without destroying themselves. Materials are being investigated that can use solar energy to split water into hydrogen and oxygen [4]. Nanotechnology is a field with numerous potential applications for today, and wholly revolutionary advances are possible.

Computational materials science is a field likely to have significant impact on scientific progress and economic growth [4]. Computational technologies will need to be researched in order to efficiently design the advanced materials that can meet various challenges in materials design, such as handling extreme environments, engineering materials down to the nanoscale, photocatalysts that function with natural sunlight, catalysts for the synthesis of new fuels, and designer fluids. Experimentally optimizing these materials is impossible, as billions upon billions of materials would need to be investigated. This necessitates the use of computational tools to efficiently sift through the parameter space for optimal materials.

Private industry has been a pioneer in the design of new materials using computational tools. The methodology of Integrated Computational Materials Engineering uses computational tools to predict the properties of substances from a fundamental molecular and atomic level. This methodology has greatly reduced the cost and time required for the approval and deployment of new materials. Ford Motor Company has developed sophisticated computational models that directly link the properties of their automotive products with their manufacturing conditions [4]. Boeing has done similar things with the design of new lightweight materials in their aircraft.

17.4   Reaction Engineering and Catalysis

"Research is what I'm doing when I don't know what I'm doing."

-Wernher von Braun

Hot fields in reaction engineering are the synthesis of biomaterials, drug delivery, conversion of biomass to liquid fuels, carbon dioxide sequestration, and hydrogen production [3]. Catalysts are also being developed for the conversion of CO_2 to fuels [4]. The abundance of water on Earth has also stimulated interest in catalysts for water-splitting into hydrogen and oxygen, a technology with huge potential impact. Industrially-important processes can have tens of thousands of simultaneous reactions, and mathematically modeling these processes is an important computational challenge [4]. In the future, chemical reactors might be much smaller than they are now, as micro-reactors have much higher (>100 fold) heat and mass transfer rates compared to normal-sized reactors. Microreactors are also much safer, since much smaller quantities of chemicals are being processed at any given instant [3].

Clean coal technologies have worldwide application. In China, 70% of energy production (as of 2006) was produced by coal, while the rest of the world only gets about 20% of its energy from coal [1], [81]. New reactor designs are being investigated which can make better use of the energy and chemicals stored in coal. The Chinese are investigating the use of thermal plasma reactors for the conversion of coal to the petrochemical precursor acetylene, which could revolutionize the plastics industry [1].

Current mathematical models used for reactor design are over fifty years old, and do not harness the great advances made in computing technology or process intensification [3]. Computational modeling will likely be a key technology in the design and synthesis of new materials [4]. Researchers have also investigated the use of 3D-printing technologies for rapid prototyping and experimental optimization of reactor geometry [82]. Alteration of the reactor geometry gives the chemical engineer direct control over the flow and mixing pattern of the reactants. It has been experimentally observed that merely switching one geometry with another can directly change the obtained product from a given chemical reaction [82].

Much of the current methodologies behind CO_2 sequestration merely focus on storing the gas, either in depleted oil reservoirs deep below the earth, or injecting it at great depths into the oceans [83]. Much of these schemes involve costly liquefaction technologies (e.g. cryogenics), or stripping of CO_2-rich streams with an amine liquid. It is questionable as to whether amine-stripping actually leads to a net reduction in released CO_2. Furthermore, oceanic injection of CO_2 can have disastrous consequences for marine life. Another idea is to make direct use of the relatively-inert CO_2 molecule by photocatalytically reacting it with water vapor to make hydrocarbon fuels [84]. By engineering the band-gap of titanium dioxide with various dopants and metal particles, it has been experimentally demonstrated that the resulting photocatalyst can reduce CO_2 to methane, branched paraffins, carbon monoxide, and hydrogen using only natural sunlight. Such a technology, if refined to the point of being commercialized, would be a revolutionary achievement, as it would suddenly transform the "waste" product of CO_2 into a new fuel source.

17.5 Defense and Counter-Terrorism

"Jihad will continue even if I am not around."

-Osama bin Laden

Research into counter-terrorism technologies is almost totally focused on materials design and material properties [85]. Knowledge of the basic chemistry of organo-actinide complexes has been applied to counter-terrorism research, mainly for the detection of toxic compounds. Laser ablation of filtered air particles has been explored for the detection of minute quantities of radioactive compounds.

International terrorism is a topic of intense government interest, mainly due to terror organizations attempting to get their hands on chemical weapons [85]. The chemistry of nerve gases, blister agents, nuclear bomb components, asphyxiants, and blood toxins, and how to defeat such threats, are the subject of intense funding. Lab-on-a-chip microfluidic devices with analysis volumes as low as 1 nanoliter have also been investigated for counter-terrorism applications [85]. There is even a scientific journal called Lab-on-a-Chip [86]. What is it about? You guessed it: how to build complete chemical laboratories on chips.

17.6 Computational Chemistry

"A huge gap exists between what we know is possible with today's machines and what we have so far been able to finish."

-Donald Knuth

Computational chemistry is the use of computers to solve the complicated quantum and statistical mechanical equations that govern the properties and interactions of chemical substances [36], [87]. It is a field of rich interest to chemical engineering, especially in the pharmaceutical and energy industries. Drug companies routinely use computational chemistry software to test the effectiveness of new drug molecules on a computer before expending resources on them in the laboratory. The availability of cheap, high-performance computing resources has vastly increased the scale of the problems that can be tackled. The Swiss pharmaceutical company Novartis recently screened over ten million compounds in nine hours using Amazon Web Services (AWS) [88]. To do this calculation internally would have cost the company $40 million to build a new supercomputer. The price using AWS? About $4,000, and only three promising compounds were found out of those 10 million. Hardware tools pioneered for use in the video game industry – specifically GPUs, or "graphics processing units") – are also being leveraged for greatly increasing the speed of calculation of these simulations [4].

It may seem strange to the layperson how chemistry can be simulated on a computer, as opposed to simply doing experiments. However, experiments are costly and time-consuming, while computing power is cheap. Mathematically, the equations governing molecular dynamics and quantum mechanics are intractable for a human to solve by hand, but are solvable using computers [89]. The primary driving force behind the computational chemistry approach to the investigation of materials is cost. Simulating the properties of a material on a computer consumes a few cents' worth of electricity – actually synthesizing it in the laboratory can cost thousands of dollars.

Computational chemistry also extends to the catalysis field, using quantum mechanical calculations [4], [36]. Chemical reactions essentially boil down to the dynamic interactions between different electron wavefunctions in close proximity to each other [37]. Currently, quantum mechanical calculations on a computer can only simulate a few atoms at a time, and yet are some of the most computationally-demanding simulations in use. Nonetheless, such calculations are invaluable for the investigation of new catalysts for performing economically-relevant reactions. Much like the drug molecules in the Novartis example, it is far cheaper to screen catalysts on a computer than to endlessly synthesize new materials and test them in the laboratory. Computational studies can greatly improve the search and design process for newer, better, cheaper catalysts [4], [37].

Aside from pharmaceuticals and catalysts, computational tools are more widely applied to the more general problem of material design, especially of advanced materials such as polymer composites and electronic metamaterials [4], [37]. A major goal in computational materials science is to start with a predefined set of desired properties (chemical, optical, electronic, magnetic, mechanical, and thermal), and be able to design a material that satisfies all of the requirements at minimum cost [37]. To make progress towards this goal, skilled mathematical modelers will be needed in the future to come up with accurate mathematical descriptions of advanced materials [4], [37], [38]. A key technology in the design process will be mathematical optimization. Borrowing from the field of process systems engineering (discussed in chapter 12), multivariable optimization has been specifically named in the Materials Genome Initiative as a key technology in the design of advanced materials [38]. A shared problem in materials synthesis and pharmaceutical research is the prediction of the existence of polymorphic compounds, a problem which requires sophisticated mathematics to solve [38].

17.7 Computational Fluid Dynamics and Reaction Modeling

"Water, water, everywhere,
And all the boards did shrink;
Water, water, everywhere,
Nor any drop to drink."

-Samuel Taylor Coleridge, *The Rime of the Ancient Mariner*

Computational fluid dynamics (CFD) is a field focused on the solution of the partial differential equations of mass and momentum that govern the flow patterns of fluids (gases and liquids). These equations are:

$$\frac{\partial \rho}{\partial t} + \nabla \cdot (\rho \mathbf{u}) = 0$$

$$\rho \left(\frac{\partial \mathbf{u}}{\partial t} + \mathbf{u} \cdot \nabla \mathbf{u} \right) = -\nabla p + \nabla \cdot \mathbf{T} + \mathbf{f}$$

Where $\mathbf{u}$ is the velocity field we are solving for, ρ is the density of the fluid, $\mathbf{T}$ is the stress tensor, and $\mathbf{f}$ is the sum of all body forces acting on all of the fluid elements in the system. Except in toy examples, it is usually impossible to solve these equations by hand and obtain an analytic solution. For real problems, such as modeling the mixing of two fluid streams, powerful computers are used to break these equations down into a large number of simpler sub-problems, which can then be solved repeatedly to obtain the correct final solution.

CFD is a necessity these days for the manufacture of chemical products where fluid flow patterns govern the quality of the final product – especially if there are significant heat transfer effects or chemical reactions occurring as well [36]. Chemical-vapor deposition reactors for manufacturing semiconductors have been modeled using this approach [36]. Solution of these equations becomes dramatically more difficult when the fluids in question are responsive to electromagnetic fields. The modeling of magnetic fluids and electrically-charged fluids is an active research field. Likewise if the fluids exhibit non-Newtonian or viscoelastic properties.

18 Process Systems Engineering and Optimization in Chemical Engineering

18.1 Introduction

"We are all experts in our own little niches."

-Alex Trebek

This is a research area I am partial to, and so I will write more about it than the other sections. After all, my own doctoral research was on the mathematical optimization of pharmaceutical crystallization processes, which was also the focus of our research group at Purdue [61], [62], [90]–[97]. And yet even with an extended amount of writing, I will barely scratch the surface of this highly intriguing field. The major centers for optimization research as it relates to chemical engineering are the departments of Carnegie-Mellon University in Pittsburgh, Pennsylvania, the Imperial College of London, the University of Wisconsin-Madison in Madison, Wisconsin, and Purdue University in West Lafayette, Indiana. Much of the material cited in this section has been authored by alumni of these research groups. The knowledge in this chapter is directly applicable to a wide array of real-world problems facing a multitude of different industries, ranging from chemicals manufacture to the financial sector. To get a full appreciation of the applications in this chapter, I have included a brief "crash course" in optimization theory that ought to be basic enough to be understandable by the advanced high school student.

18.2 Why Learn All that Mathematics?

"All science requires mathematics."

-Roger Bacon

It is understandable why most people went through middle school and high school dreading math class. Few things, other than perhaps terrorism and pedophilia, have worse public relations than math. Unless you have direct exposure at a young age to the uses of mathematics, like a parent with a high-paying, math-intensive job, you are unlikely to have much appreciation for its potential applications. Furthermore, your situation is different when you're in K-12 school. You do mathematics and nothing comes of it. There's no reward or payoff other than getting a "Job well done!" from your teachers, and forestalling the wrath of your parents from getting bad grades.

It doesn't work that way in the real world. Should you go on to pursue and succeed in a mathematically demanding specialty, there are many employers who will be interested in talking to you. I'm a case example. My own skills at math are what puts food in my fridge and a roof over my head. If you're good at mathematics, and possess a wide breadth and depth of knowledge on the subject, you can have a lucrative and rewarding career. One such sub-field of chemical engineering that is big on mathematics is process systems engineering (PSE), which is mainly concerned with optimizing chemical processes. You can make a lot of money doing optimization. Much like how top corporate attorneys can charge obscene fees to negotiate huge mergers, if you can increase profits of a big company by even a fraction of 1 percent, you're worth a big paycheck to them. The skills I'm discussing in this chapter are in high demand; companies not even related to chemicals manufacturing are on the hunt for people with them. Several graduate students from the department back at Purdue ended up working for Amazon, and at least one ended up working for Intel – all due to their expertise in large-scale mathematical optimization.

18.3   Definition and Uses of Process Systems Engineering

"Mathematics is a more powerful instrument of knowledge than any other that has been bequeathed to us by human agency."

-Rene Descartes

Process systems engineering is the application of advanced mathematics from the fields of operations research, risk management, artificial intelligence, applied mathematics, control theory, and computer science to solve extremely large planning, decision, and optimization problems in the chemical processing and energy industries, among other places. How "big" is big? Currently, state-of-the-art optimization solvers can handle millions of variables and hundreds of thousands of constraints [98], [99]. The scale of problems reflect the scale of applications, such as enterprise-wide optimization [100]. Workers in PSE use these sophisticated mathematical techniques to solve a whole host of complicated problems in chemical engineering [81]. The overarching goal of using all this mathematics is to ensure that chemical products are produced with the least energy, least materials, and least cost. For the remainder of this chapter, though, we will confine our discussion solely to the topic of optimization. This is due partly for reasons of brevity, and also due to the intense focus on optimization among PSE practitioners.

18.4 Optimization and the Chemical Engineer

"... the general who wins a battle makes many calculations in his temple ere the battle is fought. The general who loses a battle makes but few calculations beforehand. Thus do many calculations lead to victory, and few calculations to defeat: how much more no calculation at all!"

-Sun Tzu, *The Art of War*

Chemical engineers are frequently bedeviled by all sorts of hard questions, such as "How much?", "How many?", "At what time?", "In what fashion?" and "Where at?" This is a natural consequence of the fact that in our models we often end up with more variables than we have equations, and thus the variables we have control over are up to us to decide the value of. But not all choices of variables make any economic sense, or are even possible to enact in practice. A given pump can only output so much flow. Storage tanks only hold so much material. Motors can only handle so many RPM. Pressurized vessels can only withstand up to some maximum pressure – and so on and so forth for a whole variety of equipment.

These kinds of choices are found at every stage of chemicals manufacturing, whether it is finding the best recipe, synthesizing the best flowsheet for manufacturing the chemical, the general operation of the plant, or to the logistical supply chain that ships the chemicals to the customers. The difference between good choices and bad ones can mean being driven out of business. To confound matters further, the phenomena that chemical engineers study is so mathematically complicated, that the optimal strategy is not obvious or is completely counterintuitive.

And what are we to do when uncertainty presents its grim visage? It may appear to be economically optimal to produce five hundred tons per day of a given chemical, but what if demand only pans out to be three hundred tons per day? What if our experimental parameters have significant uncertainty? How will that affect the process equipment, and the plant as a whole? Can we still manufacture a product that is "on-spec" in the teeth of uncertainty? What is the cost impact of this uncertainty? What is the return on investment from reducing this uncertainty? These are the kinds of questions a process systems engineer tries to answer using optimization.

18.5 What is this Thing Called "Optimization"?

"For since the fabric of the universe is most perfect and the work of a most wise Creator, nothing at all takes place in the universe in which some rule of maximum or minimum does not appear."

-Leonhard Euler

Mathematical optimization is the process of building a mathematical model of a system, and then manipulating certain variables that compose the model to identify the set of variables that minimize or maximize some quantity. There are three components to any optimization problem [101]–[103]:

- An "objective function," J, which gives us some idea of how good of a job our chosen strategy is doing. By convention, the goal is typically to minimize J, though maximizing J is the same as minimizing the negative of J. There are a whole host of ideas as to what ought to define J, such as minimizing cost, maximizing profits, minimizing pollution, and many others of concern to chemical engineers.

- A set of "decision variables." We need to know what variables we actually have control over to do the optimization. Plugging in different values of the decision variables alters the value of J, with the goal of minimizing it.

- A set of "constraint equations." If we were to minimize J without any constraints, we would likely wind up with a nonsense answer. What gives mathematical optimization its usefulness is the ability to mathematically incorporate constraints into the problem formulation. This set of constraint expressions defines the permissible limits of our decision variables. These expressions are either in the form of equalities, inequalities, or in terms of a discrete, countable set of allowed values (e.g. $\{0, 1, 2..., \}$).

Common constraints are budget, total raw material supply, warehouse capacity, storage tank capacity, maximum permissible pollution emissions, minimum required chemical reaction selectivity, minimum required chemical reaction conversion, safety-related constraints, maximum number of allowed actions, lower and upper bounds on all of the decision variables, and a multitude of others.

Frequently in engineering we are confronted by decisions that can only have a discrete value. Constraining certain values to the positive integers is useful for problems that include discrete quantities as part of the problem formulation (e.g. how many pieces of equipment, how many personnel, how many atoms, etc). For example, if we were trying to optimize a series of distillation columns for separating petrochemicals, how could we possibly have "half" of a distillation column? How could we have "three-quarters" of a worker assigned to operate a piece of process equipment? Fractions do not make logical, physical sense for the choices of these variables, and so these quantities can only be discrete integer values.

The constraints are an especially important part of the problem. The software used to actually perform the minimization is not very intelligent, and is very much like water finding a leak for you – you don't know where the leak came from, but you know a leak exists because of the puddle on the floor. If you leave out an important constraint, then your problem will simply be "unbounded" and the software will return the worthless value of negative infinity for you, or some other infeasible result. The incorporation of the correct constraints along with the model equations forces the optimizer to follow reality – or at least, what the model is claiming reality is – and prevents the minimization of J from zooming down to an infeasible result every time.

18.6 The Confusing Term "Mathematical Programming"

"Aim for brevity while avoiding jargon."

-Edsger Dijkstra

There is one issue I want to clear up that is likely to be a source of great confusion to a young person. The term "programming" is widely used in textbooks and the optimization literature, but it has a different meaning in this context than what laypersons are normally accustomed to. When laypeople hear the term "programming," they think of writing code for a computer to execute. Further confusion is added by the fact that "mathematical programming" is today almost wholly performed using computers. However, the word "programming" has a more general meaning from the pre-computer days, meaning "to schedule of a set of actions." This is how the act of writing code on a computer acquired the term "programming," since that is exactly what computer code is – an ordered list of actions for a computer to execute. We are concerned in this chapter with the phrase "mathematical programming," which has nothing directly to do with computers. Mathematical programming is the use of mathematics to find the best possible program for a given task – that is, the best ordered set of actions to take to accomplish some objective. It is synonymous with "mathematical optimization."

18.7 Mathematical Formulation of an Optimization Problem

"In mathematics, you don't understand things. You just get used to them."

-John von Neumann

As stated before, a trio of components is needed to define a mathematical programming problem: an objective function, a mathematical model of the process, and a full list of all the constraints. But what does such a problem actually look like when expressed mathematically? The basic problem statement is:

$$\min J = f(x, y)$$

Subject to the constraints:

$$g_1(x, y) \leq 0$$
$$g_2(x, y) \leq 0$$
$$\vdots$$
$$g_N(x, y) \leq 0$$
$$h_1(x, y) = 0$$
$$h_2(x, y) = 0$$
$$\vdots$$
$$h_M(x, y) = 0$$
$$y \in [0, 1, 2, ...]$$

Let's discuss how to read these peculiar statements.

- The word "min" in the first equation means our goal is to minimize J,

- J (a function of both x and y) is the aforementioned objective function,

- x is the vector of continuous decision variables,

- y is the vector of integer decision variables,

- the vector $g(x,y)$ defines a list of N nonlinear inequality constraints,

- the vector $h(x,y)$ defines a list of M nonlinear equality constraints, and

- the last set of constraints confining *y* to the natural numbers is a reflection of the fact that many decision variables do not make sense when taking fractional values.

Our choices of the decision variables, *x* and *y*, must make all of these constraint statements true. There is no limit to the number of constraints a problem can have, and no limit to the number of decision variables contained within the vectors *x* and *y*. Constraints can be non-obviously redundant, and poorly-formulated problems can have mutually-exclusive constraints that render the problem mathematically unsolvable. For complicated problems with a large number of nonlinear constraints, proving that a feasible solution even exists becomes difficult [104].

The constraints collectively define the "feasible region" of the decision space. A visual example of a feasible region is shown in illustration 1 below, though usually there are so many variables and constraints that the feasible region is impossible to meaningfully visualize.

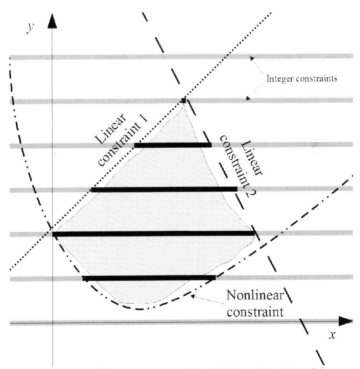

Illustration 1: A pictorial representation of a feasible region defined by several types of constraints on the continuous variables x and integer variables y. The gray region

defines a pseudo-feasible region enclosed by the two linear constraints and the nonlinear (curved) constraint. The integer constraints on y are the gray horizontal lines. The only set of ordered pairs of (x,y) that are totally feasible are the black lines within the gray region.

While this problem statement looks utterly detached from a problem in chemical engineering, this reveals the great task of the chemical engineer: to take a problem statement composed of subjective, imprecise English words, and translate it into the mathematical framework necessary to perform optimization. This is a difficult skill to grasp, but the problem must be reduced to this form before computational solver software can be put to work finding the answer.

This problem is one of the most difficult mathematics problems a chemical engineer could ever be asked to solve. The correct label for this kind of problem is a "mixed-integer nonlinear programming" problem, or MINLP. Despite the great difficulty of this type of problem, it is a frequent occurrence in chemical engineering and the business world [98].

MINLP problems require sophisticated computer programs to find the minimum. There are many different methods that can be used, such as by iteratively minimizing a simpler function guaranteed to underestimate the original problem, and a whole host of techniques based on random sampling of the decision space [99], [104]. If the problem can be approximated as entirely linear, the problem becomes a "mixed-integer linear programming problem," or MILP, which can be solved with off-the-shelf software (GNU Octave, discussed in section 1, comes with the solver "GLPK" that can handle MILP problems). High-end commercial solver software, such as CPLEX, XPRESS and Gurobi, can handle large-scale optimization problems, but cost tens of thousands of dollars to license [29], [105]–[107]. Further discussion of these techniques is beyond the scope of this work, though the interested reader can read up on solution methods in any optimization textbook as well as literature sources [29], [98], [99], [102]–[104], [108]–[112].

18.8 Local Versus Global Optimization

"In whose hand are the depths of the earth, The peaks of the mountains are His also."

-The Old Testament, Psalm 95:4

Ignoring for the effect of constraints, a "local minimum" is a region where the objective function resembles a bowl-shape with a minimum at the bottom, but is not the "deepest bowl" in the feasible region[19]. A "global minimum" is the point corresponding to the lowest possible value of the objective function within the feasible region. Multiple local minima and multiple global minima are also possible. Illustration 2 below shows the two cases.

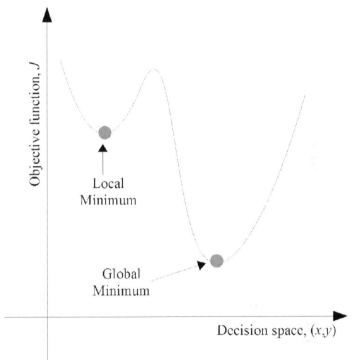

Illustration 2: Local versus global minima. For simplicity, the decision space is represented by a single axis.

Logically, we desire the absolute best possible solution for a given problem. The best solution is given by finding the global minimum,

---

[19] In the language of multivariate calculus, a "local minimum" is a point where the gradient is zero, the Hessian matrix is positive definite, but the function value of the objective function is *not* the lowest possible value it could be within the feasible region. When constraints are factored in, the more complicated Karush-Kuhn-Tucker (KKT) conditions are needed for a point to be considered a local minimum. Further discussion of the KKT conditions is beyond the scope of this work.

and sometimes the difference between the global minimum and the second-best solution can be millions of dollars, or calculating a prediction that doesn't match experimental observations. This process of finding the global minimum to a problem is known as "global optimization." In the case of illustration 2, it is easy to visually find where the global minimum lies because there are only two axes on the plot. Chemical engineers are rarely spoiled by such easy problems in practice. How are you supposed to visually find the global minimum to a problem with 5000 continuous variables, 250 integer variables, and 2000 constraints? Adjiman et. al. describes a pumping network design optimization problem with thirty-seven distinct local minima [109]. On the same note, global optimization problems are common in computational studies of molecular structure, since molecules preferentially assume a configuration of minimum energy. Floudas et. al. discusses the minimization of a single-variable pseudo-ethane molecular potential energy function of the form [104]:

$$f_1(x) = A(x) + B(x) + C(x) + D(x) + E(x) + F(x)$$

$$A(x) = \frac{588600}{\left[g_1(r_0,\theta) - 2\left(\sin^2(\theta)\cos\left(x - \frac{2\pi}{3} \right) - \cos^2(\theta) \right)r_0^2 \right]^6}$$

$$B(x) = -\frac{1079.1}{\left(g_1(r_0,\theta) - 2\left(\sin^2(\theta)\cos\left(x - \frac{2\pi}{3} \right) - \cos^2(\theta) \right)r_0^2 \right)^3}$$

$$C(x) = \frac{600800}{\left[g_1(r_0,\theta) - 2\left(\sin^2(\theta)\cos(x) - \cos^2(\theta) \right)r_0^2 \right]^6}$$

$$D(x) = -\frac{1071.5}{\left(g_1(r_0,\theta) - 2\left(\sin^2(\theta)\cos(x) - \cos^2(\theta) \right)r_0^2 \right)^3}$$

$$E(x) = \frac{481300}{\left[g_1(r_0,\theta) - 2\left(\sin^2\left(\theta + \frac{2\pi}{3} \right)\cos(x) - \cos^2(\theta) \right)r_0^2 \right]^6}$$

$$F(x) = -\frac{1064.6}{\left(g_1(r_0,\theta) - 2\left(\sin^2\left(\theta + \frac{2\pi}{3} \right)\cos(x) - \cos^2(\theta) \right)r_0^2 \right)^3}$$

$$g_1(r_0,\theta) = 3r_0^2 - 4\cos(\theta)r_0^2$$

The objective is to globally minimize $f_1(x)$ with respect to the molecule's dihedral angle, x, over $[0°, 360°]$; r_0 is the covalent bond length (1.54 Angstroms), and θ is the covalent bond angle (109.5°). The presence of a multitude of sine and cosine functions means that this function will be riddled with local minima, making the global minimum difficult to find other than by random chance or visual inspection of the graph over the domain of x.

Standard solver algorithms often get "trapped" in local minima, and totally avoid finding the global minimum. Sophisticated mathematics and powerful computers are needed to find solutions to these difficult problems. Global optimization is a research field with great practical and scientific interest, and in fact, there is an entire mathematical journal devoted to the topic – The Journal of Global

Optimization [113].

18.9 An Application: The Optimal Design of Refrigerant Molecules

"If it weren't for the fact that the TV set and the refrigerator are so far apart, some of us wouldn't get any exercise at all."

-Joey Adams

There are legions of examples in the PSE literature of optimization problems solved using various techniques. An example can give the reader some idea as to the scale of problems being tackled today in chemical engineering, which might give them some idea as to what scale of problems are going to be on the horizon ten years from now.

In this section we discuss how optimization can be used to design better refrigerants. Other noteworthy applications of optimization include the optimal design of distillation column arrays, the optimal design of complicated molecular structures such as proteins, the planning of oilfield investments, and the optimal control of microwave fields in the cooking of food [99], [104], [110], [114], [115].

Computers have been used since about the late 1990's for optimal molecular design, where properties of substances are estimated computationally, and some objective function is minimized to converge upon a substance with the desired properties. Desired properties are generally dictated by economic and business considerations. The general idea is to select a variety of molecular functional groups to add to the designed molecule, and then use a special function called a "group contribution method" to predict various properties of the substance. Group contribution methods can predict all sorts of properties on the basis of a molecule's functional groups, such as density, boiling point, and viscosity. It would be economically infeasible to experimentally test all of the substances the computer inspects, since with only ten functional groups the number of molecular combinations reaches into the millions. In this section, we will explore how better refrigerants can be identified using optimization. We borrow heavily from Chapter 2 of Seader, Seider, and Lewin for this example [116]. More sophisticated methods of property prediction, such as Monte-Carlo methods, are beyond the scope of our discussion here.

A refrigerant is the working fluid in a vapor-compression refrigeration cycle, much like the one used in your home's refrigerator. In the standard vapor-compression refrigeration cycle, a compressor does work on the refrigerant in the gas phase, elevating it to a high temperature and pressure. The gas then moves to the condenser – the coils on the back of the refrigerator – where it returns to the liquid state, rejecting heat to the surroundings. It is then throttled through a valve, where it then moves into the evaporator coils in the interior of the refrigerator to chill the food inside. The cycle repeats itself as long as the refrigerator has electrical power.

Thermodynamics tells us that the ideal performance of a refrigerator is independent of the refrigerant used; there is no magic substance that will increase the device's efficiency over another substance. This might make the reader wonder at the purpose of this section: if we cannot improve the refrigerator's efficiency through our choice of refrigerant, then what is the purpose of thinking up new refrigerants? The rebuttal to this is that there are a multitude of other aspects of refrigerants that affect their usefulness. Some molecules make great refrigerants, but might be better used as chemical weapons due to their toxicity. Others tend to go "boom." Some will try to polymerize within the device. Instead of mindlessly experimenting with thousands of refrigerants, what if we could computationally design a refrigerant that avoided these problems?

Among other measures of performance is the refrigerant's reactivity towards ozone, the O_3 molecule. Ozone is an important part of the Earth's atmosphere, which chlorofluorocarbon (CFC) refrigerants love to gobble up. One such method of designing refrigerants is to computationally select a refrigerant with the minimum reactivity towards ozone. Seider, Seader, and Lewin discusses such an optimization problem [116]. The optimization attempts to minimize reactivity towards ozone by building a refrigerant molecule while subject to a set of constraint equations. The objective function – for the case of molecules with a single carbon atom – is given by:

$$ODP = 0.585602 \times n_{Cl}^{-0.0035} \times \exp\left(\frac{M}{238.563}\right)$$

Where ODP is the "ozone depletion potential," n_{Cl} is the number of chlorine atoms in the molecule, and M is the molecule's total molecular weight. Before we can write the constraint equations, a variety of auxiliary variables need to be computed. The auxiliary equations are numerous and formidable:

The trial molecule's normal boiling point – temperature at which it boils at 1 atmosphere, or 101,325 Pascals – is calculated using:

$$T_b = 198.2 + \sum_{i=1}^{N} T_{b_i} n_i$$

The critical temperature is given by:

$$T_c = T_b \left[0.584 + 0.965 \sum_{i=1}^{N} T_{c_i} n_i - \left(\sum_{i=1}^{N} T_{c_i} n_i \right)^2 \right]^{-1}$$

The critical pressure is given by:

$$P_c = \left(0.113 + 0.0032 \times \sum_{i=1}^{N} n_i - \sum_{i=1}^{N} P_{c_i} n_i \right)^{-2}$$

Where T_b is the boiling point in Kelvin, n_i is the number of atoms in the ith functional group, $T_{b,i}$ is the group contribution to the boiling point for the ith functional group, $T_{c,i}$ is the group contribution to the critical temperature for the ith functional group, P_c is the critical pressure in bar, and $P_{c,i}$ is the group contribution to the critical pressure for the ith functional group.

The vapor pressure of the refrigerant is given by:

$$\ln\left(P_r^s\right) = \frac{-G\left[1 - T_r^2 + k(3 + T_r)(1 - T_r)^3\right]}{T_r}$$

$$G = 0.4835 + 0.4605 \times h$$

$$h = T_{b_r} \times \frac{\ln(P_c)}{1 - T_{b_r}}$$

$$k = \frac{\left[\dfrac{h}{G} - (1 + T_{b_r})\right]}{(3 + T_{b_r})(1 - T_{b_r})^2}$$

$$T_r = \frac{T}{T_c}$$

$$P_c = \frac{P}{P_c}$$

$$P_r^s = \frac{P^s}{P_c}$$

$$T_{b_r} = \frac{T_b}{T_c}$$

Where T_r is the reduced temperature, P_r is the reduced pressure, P_r^s is the reduced vapor pressure, P^s is the actual vapor pressure, and $T_{b,r}$ is the reduced normal boiling point.

The liquid phase heat capacity in calories/mole•Kelvin is given by:

$$c_p^{liquid} = 0.239 \sum_{i=1}^{N} c_{p,i}^{liquid} n_i$$

Where $c_{p,i}^{liquid}$ is the group contribution to the liquid phase heat capacity from the ith functional group.

The latent heat of vaporization at the normal boiling point, ΔH_v^b, in J/mol is given by:

$$\Delta H_v^b = S_{vb} T_b$$

$$S_{vb} = 44.367 + 15.33\log(T_b) + \frac{0.39137 \times T_b}{M} + \frac{0.00433 \times T_b^2}{M} - 5.627 \times 10^{-6} \times \frac{T_b^3}{M}$$

When at any temperature other than the normal boiling point:

$$\Delta H_v = \Delta H_v^b \left[\frac{1 - T_r}{1 - T_{b_r}} \right]^Q$$

$$Q = \left[\frac{0.00264 \times \Delta H_v^b}{RT_b} + 0.8794 \right]^{10}$$

Where ΔH_v is the latent heat of vaporization (J/mol) and R is the gas constant, 8.314 J/mol•K.

With the auxiliary equations out of the way, we can finally write our constraint equations:

1. We require a vapor pressure at -1.1 °C of greater than 1.4 bar:

$$P^s(-1.1^o C) \geq 1.4$$

2. We require the vapor pressure at 43.3 °C to be less than 14 bar:

$$P^s(43.3^o C) \leq 14$$

3. The enthalpy of vaporization at -1.1 °C must be greater than 18,400 J/mol:

$$\Delta H^v(-1.1^o C) \geq 18,400$$

4. The liquid phase heat capacity at 21.1 °C must be less than 32.2 calories/mole•Kelvin:

$$c_p^{liquid}(21.1^o C) \leq 32.2$$

For the sake of simplicity, we have omitted other important constraints. For example, compounds with double and triple bonds make poor choices of refrigerant due to their tendency to polymerize, and compounds formed with nitrogen and halides together can be explosive. Also, each atom in the molecule needs to satisfy the Octet Rule.

The final step is to load all of the data on each chemical group contribution into a computer solver, such as GAMS, and solve the above optimization problem to minimize ODP subject to the above four constraints computed using the auxiliary equations [117]. Using the data table on page fifty-five of Seader, Seider, and Lewin (see Table 2 below):

Table 2: Group contributions to properties required for refrigerant molecule optimization.

Functional Group	Valence	T_c	P_c	V_c	T_b	n_i	c_p^{liquid}	M
-CH$_3$	1	0.0141	-0.0012	65	23.58	4	36.8	15.04
-CH$_2$-	2	0.0189	0.0000	56	22.88	3	30.4	14.03
-CH=	3	0.0164	0.0020	41	21.74	2	21	13.02
=C=	4	0.0067	0.0043	27	18.25	1	7.36	12.01
-OH	1	0.0741	0.0112	28	92.88	2	44.8	17.01
-O-	2	0.0168	0.0015	18	22.42	1	35	16
-NH$_2$	1	0.0243	0.0109	38	73.23	3	58.6	16.03
-NH-	2	0.0295	0.0077	35	50.17	2	43.9	15.02
-N=	3	0.0169	0.0074	9	11.74	1	31	14.01
-S-	2	0.0119	0.0049	54	68.78	1	33	32.07
-SH	1	0.0031	0.0084	63	63.56	2	44.8	33.08
-F	1	0.0111	-0.0057	27	-0.03	1	17	19
-Cl	1	0.0105	-0.0049	58	38.13	1	36	35.45

The optimal pair of refrigerants, both with an ODP of exactly zero, are predicted to be sulfur difluoride (SF_2) and refrigerant HFC-152a (also known as 1,1-difluoroethane, CH_3CHF_2). With zero chlorine atoms, these refrigerants have zero ODP from the objective function above. The results suggest that these refrigerants can satisfy all of the required constraints, while having virtually no impact on the ozone layer. This example also shows the reader how there can exist multiple global optima, as both choices of refrigerant have the same objective function score. However, this example does not consider the potential for human toxicity, or how costly these two refrigerants may currently be to produce. It also does not consider what the optimal refrigerant might be for dramatically different evaporator and condenser temperatures.

18.10 Future Issues in Process Systems Engineering

"The things I once imagined would be my greatest achievements were only the first steps toward a future I can only begin to fathom."

-Wizards of the Coast

Improvements in computer hardware have greatly increased the scale of the problems that can be tackled with optimization. A major challenge in the deployment of an optimization technology is keeping the underlying model consistently up-to-date with accurate information regarding the system it is attempting to model. For extremely large problems that need to be repeatedly solved – several hundred thousand variables or more – this can lead to a serious data management problem [29]. Modern information technology tools will likely be an important part of future optimization endeavors.

Vast differences in time and length scale can separate various aspects of an optimization problem. For instance: year-scale for investment strategizing, month-scale planning based on seasonal trends in demand, week-scale for planning production targets, day-scale for the day, and hour/minute scale for process control purposes. It is likely impossible to completely optimize at all of these scales simultaneously, so a layered approach is often used. Length scales are also widely varying, such as molecular-scale lengths when considering chemical reactions, to plant-scale lengths when considering the totality of the operation of an entire chemical plant, and all the way to inter-site distances, where manufacturing and supply chain operations can span entire continents and cross vast oceans.

19 References

[1] Y. Jin and Y. Cheng, "Chemical engineering in China: Past, present and future," *AIChE J.*, vol. 57, no. 3, pp. 552–560, 2011.

[2] G. Garnier, "Grand challenges in chemical engineering," *Front. Chem.*, vol. 2, p. 17, 2014.

[3] M. P. Dudukovic, "Frontiers in Reactor Engineering," *Science*, vol. 325, no. 5941, p. 698, Aug. 2009.

[4] G. Crabtree, S. Glotzer, B. McCurdy, and J. Roberto, "Computational Materials Science and Chemistry: Accelerating Discovery and Innovation through Simulation-Based Engineering and Science," *Office of Scientific and Technical Information*, 26-Jul-2010. [Online]. Available: http://www.osti.gov/scitech/biblio/1294275-computational-materials-science-chemistry-accelerating-discovery-innovation-through-simulation-based-engineering-science. [Accessed: 18-Oct-2016].

[5] Encyclopedia Britannica, "chemical engineering," *Encyclopedia Britannica Online*. 2016.

[6] R. J. Smith and Editors of Encylopedia Britannica, "engineering," *Encyclopædia Britannica Online*, 30-Nov-2014. [Online]. Available: http://www.britannica.com/technology/engineering. [Accessed: 17-Jan-2016].

[7] NASA, "Astronaut Bio:Mae C. Jemison," *NASA*, Mar-1993. [Online]. Available: http://www.jsc.nasa.gov/Bios/htmlbios/jemison-mc.html. [Accessed: 17-Jan-2016].

[8] Fortune Magazine, "Fortune 500 - Fortune," *Fortune Magazine*, 2015. [Online]. Available: http://fortune.com/fortune500. [Accessed: 17-Jan-2016].

[9] IBISWorld, "Global Oil & Gas Exploration & Production Market Research," *IBISWorld*, Dec-2015. [Online]. Available: http://www.ibisworld.com/industry/global/global-oil-gas-exploration-production.html. [Accessed: 18-Jan-2016].

[10] Wikipedia, "List of largest oil and gas companies by revenue - Wikipedia," *Wikipedia*, 10-Oct-2016. [Online]. Available: https://en.wikipedia.org/wiki/List_of_largest_oil_and_gas_companies_by_revenue. [Accessed: 17-Oct-2016].

[11] Statista, "Pharmaceutical market worldwide revenue 2001-2014 |

Statistic," *Statista*, 2014. [Online]. Available:
http://www.statista.com/statistics/263102/pharmaceutical-market-worldwide-revenue-since-2001. [Accessed: 18-Jan-2016].

[12] Thomson Reuters, "Global pharma sales to reach $1.3 trillion," *Thomson Reuters*, 04-Aug-2015. [Online]. Available:
http://thomsonreuters.com/en/articles/2015/global-pharma-sales-reach-above-1-trillion.html. [Accessed: 17-Oct-2016].

[13] CSIMarket, "Food Processing Industry Stock Performance, Stock Quotes - CSIMarket," *CSIMarket*, 2016. [Online]. Available:
http://csimarket.com/Industry/Industry_Performance.php?ind=505. [Accessed: 18-Jan-2016].

[14] IBISWorld, "Global Paper & Pulp Mills Market Research | IBIS-World," *IBISWorld*. [Online]. Available:
http://www.ibisworld.com/industry/global/global-paper-pulp-mills.html. [Accessed: 18-Jan-2016].

[15] Statista, "Top mining companies total revenue 2002-2014," *Statista*, 2014. [Online]. Available:
http://www.statista.com/statistics/208715/total-revenue-of-the-top-mining-companies. [Accessed: 18-Jan-2016].

[16] PriceWaterhouseCoopers, "Mine 2015: The Gloves are Off," *PriceWaterhouseCoopers*, 2015. [Online]. Available:
http://www.pwc.com/gx/en/mining/publications/assets/pwc-e-and-m-mining-report.pdf. [Accessed: 18-Jan-2016].

[17] Edison Electric Institute, "Key Facts about the Electric Power Industry," *Center for Energy Workforce Development*, 2005. [Online]. Available:
http://www.cewd.org/toolkits/teacher/eeipub_keyfacts_electric_industry.pdf. [Accessed: 18-Jan-2016].

[18] US Energy Information Administration, "Electric Power Annual 2013," *Energy Information Administration*, Mar-2015. [Online]. Available: https://www.eia.gov/electricity/annual/pdf/epa.pdf. [Accessed: 18-Jan-2016].

[19] MDDI, "The U.S. Medical Device Industry: Strengths, Weaknesses, Opportunities, and Threats," *MDDI*, 12-Jan-2015. [Online]. Available: http://www.mddionline.com/article/us-medical-device-industry-swot-analysis-01-12-2015. [Accessed: 18-Jan-2016].

[20] MDDI, "Top 40 Medical Device Companies," *MDDI*, 21-Nov-2014. [Online]. Available:
http://www.mddionline.com/article/top-40-medical-device-

companies. [Accessed: 18-Jan-2016].

[21] Yahoo! Finance, "Industry Profile for Personal Care & Household Cleaning Products - Yahoo Finance," *Yahoo! Finance*, 17-Jan-2016. [Online]. Available: http://biz.yahoo.com/ic/prof/33.html. [Accessed: 18-Jan-2016].

[22] The Plastics Industry Trade Assocation, "plastics fact sheet," *The Plastics Industry Trade Assocation*, 2012. [Online]. Available: http://www.plasticsindustry.org/files/industry/facts/Plastics% 20fact%20sheet%202010%2D2011%5F1355148983205%5F1.p df. [Accessed: 18-Jan-2016].

[23] IBISWorld, "Plastic & Resin Manufacturing in the US Market Research | IBISWorld," *IBISWorld*, Nov-2015. [Online]. Available: http://www.ibisworld.com/industry/default.aspx?indid=473. [Accessed: 18-Jan-2016].

[24] New York University, "Major in Chemistry, B.S. Degree," *New York University Department of Chemistry*, 2013. [Online]. Available: http://chemistry.fas.nyu.edu/docs/IO/3771/MajorChemistryB S_as_of_F2013.pdf. [Accessed: 22-Oct-2016].

[25] College of Engineering and Applied Science | University of Colorado Boulder, "Chemical Engineering: BS Sample Curriculum," *College of Engineering and Applied Science | University of Colorado Boulder*, 2016. [Online]. Available: http://www.colorado.edu/engineering/academics/degree/chem ical-engineering/sample-curriculum. [Accessed: 22-Oct-2016].

[26] T. J. Stanley and W. D. Danko, *The Millionaire Next Door: The Surprising Secrets of America's Wealthy*. Taylor Trade Publishing, 2010.

[27] G. S. Clason, *The Richest Man in Babylon*. Signet, 2002.

[28] B. Graham, J. Zweig, and W. E. Buffett, *The Intelligent Investor: The Definitive Book on Value Investing*. HarperBusiness, 2006.

[29] I. E. Grossmann, "Advances in mathematical programming models for enterprise-wide optimization," *FOCAPO 2012*, vol. 47, pp. 2–18, Dec. 2012.

[30] A. Clarey, *Worthless - The Young Person's Indispensable Guide to Choosing the Right Major*. Paric, 2011.

[31] R. Florida, "NJIT: Features: Why Study Chemical Engineering? A Q&A with Reg Tomkins." [Online]. Available: http://www.njit.edu/features/sceneandheard/whystudychemica lengineering.php. [Accessed: 17-Jan-2016].

[32] Bureau of Labor Statistics, "Chemical Engineers," *Bureau of Labor*

Statistics, May-2014. [Online]. Available:
http://www.bls.gov/oes/current/oes172041.htm. [Accessed: 18-Jan-2016].

[33] D. Clark, "Chemical Engineering Starting Salaries Rank Among Highest in U.S.," *AICHE*, 31-May-2013. [Online]. Available: http://www.aiche.org/chenected/2013/05/chemical-engineering-starting-salaries-rank-among-highest-us. [Accessed: 18-Jan-2016].

[34] R. B. Bird, W. E. Stewart, and E. N. Lightfoot, *Transport Phenomena*. John Wiley & Sons, 2007.

[35] R. M. Felder and R. W. Rousseau, *Elementary Principles of Chemical Processes*, 3rd ed. New York: Wiley, 2000.

[36] J.-C. Charpentier, "The triplet 'molecular processes–product–process' engineering: the future of chemical engineering ?," *Festschr. Honour Dr Winn Van Swaaij*, vol. 57, no. 22–23, pp. 4667–4690, Nov. 2002.

[37] J. C. Hemminger, "Challenges at the Frontiers of Matter and Energy," U.S. Department of Energy, Nov. 2015.

[38] J. P. Holdren, "Materals Genome Initiative Strategic Plan," National Science and Technology Council, USA, Dec. 2014.

[39] Encyclopedia Britannica, "transport phenomenon," *Encyclopædia Britannica Online*, 2016. [Online]. Available: http://www.britannica.com/science/transport-phenomenon. [Accessed: 17-Jan-2016].

[40] Encyclopædia Britannica, "economy of scale," *Encyclopædia Britannica Online*, 2016. [Online]. Available: http://www.britannica.com/topic/economy-of-scale. [Accessed: 13-Jan-2016].

[41] T. Sowell, *Basic Economics: A Common Sense Guide to the Economy*, Fourth Edition. New York: Basic Books, 2011.

[42] NASA, "Navier-Stokes Equations," *NASA*, 05-May-2015. [Online]. Available: https://www.grc.nasa.gov/www/k-12/airplane/nseqs.html. [Accessed: 20-Oct-2016].

[43] Wikipedia, "Neutron transport," *Wikipedia*, 09-Oct-2016. [Online]. Available: https://en.wikipedia.org/wiki/Neutron_transport. [Accessed: 20-Oct-2016].

[44] C. L. Philip Chen and C.-Y. Zhang, "Data-intensive applications, challenges, techniques and technologies: A survey on Big Data," *Inf. Sci.*, vol. 275, pp. 314–347, Aug. 2014.

[45] J. Bausch, "Engineer vs engineer: Who has the higher IQ?," *Elec-*

tronic Products, 04-Jun-2012. [Online]. Available: http://www.electronicproducts.com/News/Engineer_vs_engin eer_Who_has_the_higher_IQ.aspx. [Accessed: 05-Feb-2016].

[46] R. de la Jara, "SAT I to IQ Estimator," *IQ Comparison Site*. [Online]. Available: http://www.iqcomparisonsite.com/SATIQ.aspx. [Accessed: 05-Feb-2016].

[47] S. Thompson, "Calculus Made Easy, 2nd Edition," *Project Gutenberg*, 2012. [Online]. Available: http://www.gutenberg.org/files/33283/33283-pdf.pdf?session_id=c0f89df248b7de32541d8129b4808fff046034 99. [Accessed: 03-Feb-2016].

[48] D. Downing, *Calculus the easy way*. Barron's Educational Series, 2006.

[49] H. Gross, "Calculus Revisited: Single Variable Calculus," *MIT OpenCourseWare*, 1970. [Online]. Available: http://ocw.mit.edu/resources/res-18-006-calculus-revisited-single-variable-calculus-fall-2010/course-introduction. [Accessed: 03-Feb-2016].

[50] M. Tennenbaum and H. Pollard, *Ordinary Differential Equations: An Elementary Textbook for Students of Mathematics, Engineering, and the Sciences*. Dover Publications, 1985.

[51] M. Lutz, *Learning python*. O'Reilly Media, Inc., 2013.

[52] Anonymous, "Math Skills - Dimensional Analysis," *Texas A&M University*. [Online]. Available: http://www.chem.tamu.edu/class/fyp/mathrev/mr-da.html. [Accessed: 17-Jan-2016].

[53] AICHE, "Choosing a College/University for Chemical Engineering | AIChE," *AICHE*, 2016. [Online]. Available: http://www.aiche.org/community/students/abet-accredited-universities. [Accessed: 17-Jan-2016].

[54] Accreditation Board for Engineering and Technology, "Find an ABET-Accredited Program | ABET," *ABET*, 2016. [Online]. Available: http://main.abet.org/aps/accreditedprogramsearch.aspx. [Accessed: 16-Sep-2016].

[55] J. Hopson, "Behavioral Game Design," *GamaSutra*, 27-Apr-2001. [Online]. Available: http://www.gamasutra.com/view/feature/131494/behavioral_g ame_design.php?page=1. [Accessed: 17-Jan-2016].

[56] D. Allen, *Getting things done: The art of stress-free productivity*. Hachette UK, 2015.

[57] Evernote, "The workspace for your life's work | Evernote," *Evernote*, 2016. [Online]. Available: https://evernote.com/. [Accessed: 06-Feb-2016].

[58] Roy Rosenzweig Center for History and New Media, "Zotero," *Zotero*, 2016. [Online]. Available: https://www.zotero.org. [Accessed: 20-Dec-2016].

[59] LastPass, "LastPass | Password Manager, Auto Form Filler, Random Password Generator & Secure Digital Wallet App," *LastPass*, 2016. [Online]. Available: https://lastpass.com. [Accessed: 06-Feb-2016].

[60] AICHE, "AICHE Student Design Competition Past Problems," *AICHE*, 2015. [Online]. Available: http://www.aiche.org/community/students/student-design-competition/past-problems. [Accessed: 01-Feb-2016].

[61] B. J. Ridder, A. Majumder, and Z. K. Nagy, "Population Balance Model-Based Multiobjective Optimization of a Multisegment Multiaddition (MSMA) Continuous Plug-Flow Antisolvent Crystallizer," *Ind. Eng. Chem. Res.*, vol. 53, no. 11, pp. 4387–4397, Feb. 2014.

[62] B. J. Ridder, A. Majumder, and Z. K. Nagy, "Parametric, Optimization-Based Study on the Feasibility of a Multisegment Antisolvent Crystallizer for in Situ Fines Removal and Matching of Target Size Distribution," *Ind. Eng. Chem. Res.*, vol. 55, no. 8, pp. 2371–2380, Mar. 2016.

[63] National Science Foundation, "Eligibility - NSF Graduate Research Fellowships Program (GRFP)," *NSF Graduate Research Fellowship Program*, 2016. [Online]. Available: https://www.nsfgrfp.org/applicants/eligibility. [Accessed: 21-Dec-2016].

[64] Reuters, "Journal Citation Reports Help," *Web of Knowledge*, 2012. [Online]. Available: http://admin-apps.webofknowledge.com/JCR/help/h_impfact.htm. [Accessed: 03-Jun-2016].

[65] M. J. Stringer, M. Sales-Pardo, and L. A. N. Amaral, "Statistical validation of a global model for the distribution of the ultimate number of citations accrued by papers published in a scientific journal," *J. Am. Soc. Inf. Sci. Technol.*, vol. 61, no. 7, pp. 1377–1385, 2010.

[66] C. Mirkin, "Mirkin Research Group," *The Mirkin Research Group*, 2016. [Online]. Available: http://mirkin-group.northwestern.edu. [Accessed: 03-Jun-2016].

[67] J. Pekny, "Advanced Process Combinatorics, Inc.," *Advanced Process Combinatorics*, 2016. [Online]. Available: http://www.combination.com. [Accessed: 03-Jun-2016].

[68] E. El Issa, "American Household Credit Card Debt Statistics: 2015 - NerdWallet," *NerdWallet*, 2015. [Online]. Available: https://www.nerdwallet.com/blog/credit-card-data/average-credit-card-debt-household. [Accessed: 29-May-2016].

[69] M. Kantrowitz, "Why the Student Loan Crisis Is Even Worse Than People Think," *Time*, 11-Jan-2016.

[70] R. Kim, "The Audacity of Occupy Wall Street," *The Nation*, 02-Nov-2011.

[71] M. Asatryan, "Nondischargeable Debts in Chapter 7 Bankruptcy," *nolo.com*, 2016. [Online]. Available: http://www.nolo.com/legal-encyclopedia/nondischargeable-debts-chapter-7-bankruptcy.html. [Accessed: 29-May-2016].

[72] Z. Elinson and D. Frosch, "Cost of Police-Misconduct Cases Soars in Big U.S. Cities," *The Wall Street Journal*, 15-Jul-2015. [Online]. Available: http://www.wsj.com/articles/cost-of-police-misconduct-cases-soars-in-big-u-s-cities-1437013834. [Accessed: 26-Dec-2016].

[73] M. Yang, "Chicago Police Settlements Cost Taxpayers $210 Million Plus Interest," *The Huffington Post*, 14-Jul-2016. [Online]. Available: http://www.huffingtonpost.com/entry/chicago-police-settlement-misconduct-210-million_us_5787f6a6e4b03fc3ee500a88. [Accessed: 26-Dec-2016].

[74] A. Caputo and J. Gorner, "Small group of Chicago police costs city millions in settlements," *Chicago Tribune*, 30-Jan-2016. [Online]. Available: http://www.chicagotribune.com/news/ct-chicago-police-misconduct-settlements-met-20160129-story.html. [Accessed: 26-Dec-2016].

[75] The Founding Fathers, "Constitution of the United States," *U.S. Constitution*, 17-Sep-1787. [Online]. Available: http://constitutionus.com. [Accessed: 21-Dec-2016].

[76] Supreme Court of the United States, "Salinas v. Texas," *SCOTUSblog*, 17-Apr-2013. [Online]. Available: http://www.scotusblog.com/case-files/cases/salinas-v-texas.

[Accessed: 21-Dec-2016].

[77] T. Bogerding, "WKSU News: Drug tests and drilling jobs are often in conflict," *WKSU*, 10-Jan-2013. [Online]. Available: http://wksu.org/news/story/34314. [Accessed: 15-Sep-2016].

[78] J. Haughton, "Engineering to Medicine: The Road Less Traveled," *AICHE*, 12-Jan-2014. [Online]. Available: http://www.aiche.org/community/sites/young-professionals-committee-ypc/blog/engineering-medicine-road-less-traveled. [Accessed: 24-Sep-2016].

[79] The Staff of Entrepreneur Media, *Start Your Own Business, Sixth Edition: The Only Startup Book You'll Ever Need*, 6th ed. Entrepreneur Media, 2015.

[80] Launch Angels, "Dartmouth Alumni Launch The Green D Fund to Invest in Dartmouth-Led Ventures," *Launch Angels*, 15-Sep-2014. [Online]. Available: http://www.launch-angels.com/press-release/dartmouth-alumni-launch-the-green-d-fund-to-invest-in-dartmouth-led-ventures. [Accessed: 15-Sep-2016].

[81] J. M. Ottino, "Chemical engineering in a complex world: Grand challenges, vast opportunities," *AIChE J.*, vol. 57, no. 7, pp. 1654–1668, 2011.

[82] M. D. Symes *et al.*, "Integrated 3D-printed reactionware for chemical synthesis and analysis," *Nat Chem*, vol. 4, no. 5, pp. 349–354, May 2012.

[83] J. C. M. Pires, F. G. Martins, M. C. M. Alvim-Ferraz, and M. Simões, "Recent developments on carbon capture and storage: An overview," *Spec. Issue Carbon Capture Storage*, vol. 89, no. 9, pp. 1446–1460, Sep. 2011.

[84] O. K. Varghese, M. Paulose, T. J. LaTempa, and C. A. Grimes, "High-Rate Solar Photocatalytic Conversion of CO2 and Water Vapor to Hydrocarbon Fuels," *Nano Lett.*, vol. 9, no. 2, pp. 731–737, Feb. 2009.

[85] W. Stevens *et al.*, "Basic Research Needs for Countering Terrorism," DOESC (USDOE Office of Science (SC)), 2002.

[86] Royal Society of Chemistry, "Lab on a Chip Home-Miniaturisation for chemistry, physics, biology, materials science and bioengineering," *Royal Society of Chemistry*, 2016. [Online]. Available: http://pubs.rsc.org/en/journals/journalissues/lc#!recentarticles&adv. [Accessed: 14-Jan-2016].

[87] SHODOR, "Overview of Computational Chemistry," *SHODOR*, 2000. [Online]. Available:

https://www.shodor.org/chemviz/overview/ccbasics.html. [Accessed: 12-Jan-2016].

[88] Amazon Web Services, *Novartis Uses AWS to Conduct 39 Years of Computational Chemistry In 9 Hours - YouTube*. 2014.

[89] K. N. Houk and P. Ha-Yeon Cheong, "Computational prediction of small-molecule catalysts," *Nature*, vol. 455, no. 7211, pp. 309–313, Sep. 2008.

[90] B. J. Ridder, A. Majumder, and Z. K. Nagy, "Population balance model based multi-objective optimization and robustness analysis of a continuous plug flow antisolvent crystallizer," *Am. Control Conf. ACC 2014*, pp. 3530–3535, Jun. 2014.

[91] B. J. Ridder, "Modeling, optimization, and sensitivity analysis of a continuous multi-segment crystallizer for production of active pharmaceutical ingredients," Dissertation, Purdue University, West Lafayette, Indiana, 2015.

[92] D. Acevedo and Z. K. Nagy, "Systematic classification of unseeded batch crystallization systems for achievable shape and size analysis," *J. Cryst. Growth*, vol. 394, pp. 97–105, May 2014.

[93] D. Acevedo, Y. Tandy, and Z. K. Nagy, "Multiobjective Optimization of an Unseeded Batch Cooling Crystallizer for Shape and Size Manipulation," *Ind. Eng. Chem. Res.*, vol. 54, no. 7, pp. 2156–2166, Feb. 2015.

[94] Y. Yang and Z. K. Nagy, "Combined Cooling and Antisolvent Crystallization in Continuous Mixed Suspension, Mixed Product Removal Cascade Crystallizers: Steady-State and Startup Optimization," *Ind. Eng. Chem. Res.*, vol. 54, no. 21, pp. 5673–5682, Jun. 2015.

[95] Y. Yang, L. Song, T. Gao, and Z. K. Nagy, "Integrated Upstream and Downstream Application of Wet Milling with Continuous Mixed Suspension Mixed Product Removal Crystallization," *Cryst. Growth Des.*, vol. 15, no. 12, pp. 5879–5885, Dec. 2015.

[96] Y. Yang, L. Song, and Z. K. Nagy, "Automated Direct Nucleation Control in Continuous Mixed Suspension Mixed Product Removal Cooling Crystallization," *Cryst. Growth Des.*, vol. 15, no. 12, pp. 5839–5848, Dec. 2015.

[97] Y. Yang, L. Song, Y. Zhang, and Z. K. Nagy, "Application of Wet Milling-Based Automated Direct Nucleation Control in Continuous Cooling Crystallization Processes," *Ind. Eng. Chem. Res.*, vol. 55, no. 17, pp. 4987–4996, May 2016.

[98] L. T. Biegler and I. E. Grossmann, "Retrospective on optimiza-

tion," *Comput. Chem. Eng.*, vol. 28, no. 8, pp. 1169–1192, Jul. 2004.

[99] I. E. Grossmann and L. T. Biegler, "Part II. Future perspective on optimization," *Comput. Chem. Eng.*, vol. 28, no. 8, pp. 1193–1218, Jul. 2004.

[100] I. Grossmann, "Enterpris-wide optimization: A new frontier in process systems engineering," *AIChE J.*, vol. 51, no. 7, pp. 1846–1857, 2005.

[101] Eudoxus Systems Ltd, "What is Mathematical Programming?," *Eudoxus Systems Ltd*, 2016. [Online]. Available: http://www.eudoxus.com/lp-training/1-what-is-mathematical-programming. [Accessed: 22-Jun-2016].

[102] K. J. Beers, *Numerical methods for chemical engineering: applications in Matlab*. Cambridge University Press, 2006.

[103] A. Ravindran, G. V. Reklaitis, and K. M. Ragsdell, *Engineering optimization: methods and applications*. John Wiley & Sons, 2006.

[104] C. A. Floudas, I. G. Akrotirianakis, S. Caratzoulas, C. A. Meyer, and J. Kallrath, "Global optimization in the 21st century: Advances and challenges," *Comput. Chem. Eng.*, vol. 29, no. 6, pp. 1185–1202, May 2005.

[105] IBM, "IBM CPLEX Optimizer," *CPLEX Optimizer*, 2016. [Online]. Available: https://www-01.ibm.com/software/commerce/optimization/cplex-optimizer. [Accessed: 17-Jun-2016].

[106] FICO, "FICO Xpress Optimization Suite," *FICO Xpress*, 2016. [Online]. Available: http://www.fico.com/en/products/fico-xpress-optimization-suite#overview. [Accessed: 17-Jun-2016].

[107] Gurobi, "Gurobi Optimization - The Best Mathematical Programming Solver," *Gurobi Optimization*, 2016. [Online]. Available: http://www.gurobi.com. [Accessed: 17-Jun-2016].

[108] R. Misener and C. A. Floudas, "GloMIQO: Global mixed-integer quadratic optimizer," *J. Glob. Optim.*, vol. 57, no. 1, pp. 3–50, 2013.

[109] C. S. Adjiman, I. P. Androulakis, and C. A. Floudas, "Global optimization of mixed-integer nonlinear problems," *AIChE J.*, vol. 46, no. 9, pp. 1769–1797, 2000.

[110] C. A. Floudas and C. E. Gounaris, "A review of recent advances in global optimization," *J Glob. Optim.*, vol. 45, no. 1, pp. 3–38, 2009.

[111] J. Nocedal and S. Wright, *Numerical optimization, series in operations*

research and financial engineering, 2nd ed. Springer-Verlag, 2006.

[112] D. P. Bertsekas, "Nonlinear programming," 1999.

[113] Springer, "Journal of Global Optimization - Springer," *Springer*, 2016. [Online]. Available: http://link.springer.com/journal/10898. [Accessed: 17-Jun-2016].

[114] J. A. Caballero and I. E. Grossmann, "Optimal synthesis of thermally coupled distillation sequences using a novel MILP approach," *Comput. Chem. Eng.*, vol. 61, pp. 118–135, Feb. 2014.

[115] J. R. Banga, E. Balsa-Canto, C. G. Moles, and A. A. Alonso, "Improving food processing using modern optimization methods," *Trends Food Sci. Technol.*, vol. 14, no. 4, pp. 131–144, Apr. 2003.

[116] W. D. Seider, J. D. Seader, and D. R. Lewin, *Product and process design principles: synthesis, analysis, and evaluation*, 2nd ed. Wiley, 2004.

[117] GAMS Development Corporation, "GAMS Home Page," *GAMS*, 2016. [Online]. Available: https://www.gams.com. [Accessed: 04-Jul-2016].

Made in the USA
Monee, IL
13 December 2022

21524114R00099